Title Page

Dollars and Sense: How Fi Mek Money Work Fi Yuh

(Money Mek Wi Talk – Book 1)

📖 **By Marvin Buckley**

📌 **Publisher:** Shark Solutions Limited
🎨 **Cover Design & Layout:** AI Assisted

Copyright Page

📌 **Published by:** Shark Solutions Limited
📍 **Kingston, Jamaica**
✉ **Contact:** patwah@sharksolutions.info

✓ **Paperback ISBN: 978-976-659-066-6**
✓ **eBook ISBN: 978-976-659-067-3**
✓ **Audiobook ISBN: 978-976-659-068-0**

📌 **First Edition: 2024**

Table of Contents

Copyright Page

Dedication

Acknowledgments

Preface

Introduction: Why Money Matter fi Wi People

Part 1: The Foundation – Understanding Money & Mindset

Basics a Money Management – Start Small, Think Big

Investment 101 – Mek Money Work Fi Yuh

Understanding Di Jamaican Banking System

Using Loans an Credit Wisely – Mek Debt Work Fi Yuh

Part 2: Building Wealth & Securing Your Future

Real Estate an Land Ownership – Secure Yuh Future Wid Property

Protecting Yuh Wealth – Insurance an Estate Planning Fi Secure Yuh Legacy

Long-Term Financial Strategies – Building Wealth Fi Generations

Di Right Mindset Fi Wealth Building – Stay Focused an Disciplined

Giving Back – Building Wealth Fi Yuhself an Yuh Community

Part 3: Advanced Strategies for Financial Growth

Embracing Technology Fi Wealth Building inna Di Digital Age

Managing Risk – Protecting Yuh Wealth Wid Smart, Calculated Decisions

Creating a Financial Legacy – Securing Wealth Fi Di Next Generation

Cash Flow Control – How to Manage Yuh Money Properly

Avoiding Money Traps – Understanding Bad Debt

Smart Borrowing – How to Use Debt to Build Wealth

The Magic of Compound Interest – Why Saving Alone Isn't Enough

Investing 101 – Making Your Money Work for You

Financial Freedom – How to Plan for Early Retirement

Protecting Your Wealth – Understanding Insurance & Estate Planning

Part 4: Legacy & Generational Wealth

Legacy and Generational Wealth – Mek Sure Yuh Money Outlive Yuh

Back Matter

Glossary

References

About the Author

Index

Dedication

✱ To everyone striving for financial freedom.

This book is for you—the hustler, the dreamer, the parent, the youth who refuse to settle. **Money mek wi talk, but knowledge a di real power.**

Special mention to **Chinelle Spencer, FCCA, CA**—a visionary leader in global asset management and public accounting, whose expertise and dedication to financial excellence inspire us all.

Acknowledgments

Special thanks to:

- **Uncle Roy** *(fictional character, real-life wisdom)*
- **Mi family and friends** who always push me to think bigger
- **Chinelle Spencer, FCCA, CA**—for her unparalleled guidance and support in financial management and asset protection
- **Di community of financial warriors** who believe in generational wealth
- **Jamaica and di Caribbean**—we full of potential, and it's time fi claim it

Big up everybody who support financial literacy, empowerment, and building legacy. Dis journey just start!

Preface

Money is a powerful tool that can shape our lives, communities, and futures. Yet, for many of us, it remains a source of stress, confusion, and limitations. Growing up in the vibrant culture of Jamaica, we've witnessed firsthand the struggles and triumphs that come with managing finances in a world where opportunities often seem scarce.

"Dollars and Sense: How Fi Mek Money Work Fi Yuh" was born out of a desire to bridge the gap between financial literacy and our rich Jamaican heritage. This book is not just about numbers and budgets; it's about stories—our stories, your stories, and the shared experiences that weave us together as a people.

Through the journey of Marcus, Selene, and their community, we explore the challenges that many of us face: from living paycheck to paycheck, grappling with debt, encountering unexpected hardships, to the thrill of entrepreneurship and the pursuit of financial freedom. It's a narrative that reflects the resilience, wisdom, and ingenuity inherent in Jamaican culture.

Our aim is to provide a comprehensive guide that intertwines practical financial advice with engaging storytelling. By infusing authentic Patwah dialogue and cultural references, we hope to make complex financial concepts accessible and relatable. We believe that when knowledge is shared in a way that resonates with our daily lives, it becomes not just information, but a catalyst for change.

Whether you're just starting your financial journey, seeking to improve your money management skills, or aspiring to build generational wealth, this book offers insights and strategies tailored for you. It's about empowering ourselves to take control of our finances, break cycles of poverty, and create a legacy that outlives us.

As you turn these pages, we invite you to see yourself in Marcus's story, to learn from his challenges, and to be inspired by his triumphs. Let's embark on this journey together, embracing the wisdom of our roots while carving out a prosperous future.

Remember, every mickle mek a muckle—every little bit counts. It's time to mek money work fi we, di Jamaican way.

With respect and solidarity,

Marvin Buckley

Introduction: Why Money Matter Fi Wi People

Di Roots of Resilience

In the heart of Jamaica, from the bustling streets of Kingston to the tranquil shores of Montego Bay, there's a rhythm that pulses through the veins of the island—a rhythm of resilience, hope, and aspiration. Yet, beneath the vibrant culture and the irie vibes, many of us grapple with financial struggles that weigh heavy on our daily lives.

Money matters fi wi people not just because it buys necessities, but because it represents possibilities—the chance to uplift ourselves, support our families, and contribute to our communities. It's about breaking free from the limitations that have held us back for generations and claiming the opportunities that allow us to thrive.

A Shared Experience

We've all heard stories or lived through moments when di money run out before di month does, when unexpected expenses throw our lives into disarray, or when dreams are deferred because the resources just aren't there. These experiences are common threads that connect us, highlighting the need for a deeper understanding of how to manage, grow, and protect our finances.

The Inspiration Behind the Book

This book was inspired by the real-life challenges and triumphs faced by countless Jamaicans. It's a reflection of the market vendor who saves diligently to send her children to school, the young entrepreneur hustling to turn his passion into a successful business, and the families striving to build a better future despite economic hardships.

Through the lens of characters like Marcus and Selene, we delve into the complexities of financial management within our cultural context. Their stories echo the realities many of us face and offer insights into how we can navigate the financial landscape with wisdom and confidence.

Bridging Di Gap

Financial literacy isn't just about understanding dollars and cents; it's about empowerment. It's about knowing how to make informed decisions, planning for di future, and leveraging opportunities that come our way. Yet, traditional financial advice often feels disconnected from our lived experiences.

By blending practical financial strategies with authentic Jamaican storytelling, we aim to bridge that gap. We want to present information in a way that feels accessible, relatable, and actionable. After all, when advice is grounded in familiarity, it's more likely to take root and flourish.

Our Cultural Wealth

Jamaica is rich—not just in natural beauty or cultural exports like reggae music and athletics—but in the ingenuity and tenacity of its people. We have a legacy of making much out of little, of turning struggles into songs, and hardships into stories of triumph.

This book celebrates that spirit. It acknowledges the systemic challenges we face—be it limited access to financial services, economic inequities, or generational cycles of poverty—but it also highlights the power within us to overcome them.

Why Money Management is Crucial Now More Than Ever

In an increasingly globalized world, opportunities for wealth creation are both vast and competitive. Technology has opened doors to new markets, investments, and income streams. However, without the knowledge of how to navigate these waters, we risk being left behind.

Moreover, the economic shocks from global events can have profound impacts on our local economy. Building financial resilience isn't just a personal goal; it's a community imperative. By strengthening our individual financial positions, we collectively contribute to the economic stability and growth of our nation.

What to Expect in This Book

Over the course of this book, we'll journey with Marcus and Selene as they face financial challenges, learn valuable lessons, and apply practical strategies to transform their situation. Each chapter tackles a specific aspect of financial management—from budgeting and saving to investing and legacy building.

You'll find:

- **Engaging Stories:** Situations that mirror real-life experiences, bringing financial concepts to life.
- **Authentic Dialogue:** Conversations in authentic Patwah, capturing the nuances of our language and culture.
- **Practical Advice:** Actionable steps and challenges that you can implement in your own life.
- **Cultural Insights:** Reflections on how our unique Jamaican context influences our financial decisions.

Join Di Movement

"Dollars and Sense: How Fi Mek Money Work Fi Yuh" is more than a book—it's a movement towards financial empowerment. It's about taking control of our narratives, breaking barriers, and building a foundation of wealth that honors our past while paving the way for future generations.

So, whether you're a seasoned professional, a hustling entrepreneur, a student, or someone simply seeking better financial footing, this book is for you. Let's embark on this journey together, embracing the wisdom of our ancestors and the possibilities of our future.

Remember, it's not just about making money; it's about making money work for we.

Let di journey begin.

About the Author:

Marvin Buckley

Marvin Buckley is a Jamaican entrepreneur dedicated to helping people achieve financial independence. With real-life experience building businesses, investing, and teaching financial literacy, Marvin believes in making financial knowledge accessible through relatable, easy-to-apply lessons.

🔥 **Connect With Marvin:**

📚 **More Books:** amazon.com/author/marvin-buckley

📖 **Medium Blog:**
https://medium.com/@Real_Jamaican_Patois_or_Patwah

🎓 **Free Course:** patwah.unschooler.me

✉ **For business inquiries, workshops, and collaborations:**

Email: patwah@sharksolutions.info

PART 1: DI FOUNDATION (Understanding Money & Mindset)

Chapter 1: Why Money Matters Fi Wi People—The Roots of Resilience

The Debt Collector's Knock

The humid air hung heavy in the tiny apartment, pressing down like an unwelcome burden. The distant rumble of thunder hinted at an approaching storm, but inside, a tempest of a different kind was already brewing. Eight-year-old Marcus sat at the unsteady kitchen table, his small hands clutching a stubby pencil as he sketched the sleek lines of a car—his dream escape from a reality that often felt suffocating. The single flickering bulb overhead cast wavering shadows, turning the cracked walls into a canvas of shifting shapes.

From his seat, Marcus could see his mother, Maria, standing by the narrow window. She parted the threadbare curtain just enough to peer outside, her dark eyes scanning the dimly lit street below. The scent of rain mingled with the aroma of simmering rice, but even that comfort was overshadowed by the tension that gripped the room.

Maria's heart pounded in her chest, each beat echoing like a drum in her ears. *Should we hide?* she wondered. *Pretend we're not home?* But where could they go? The weight of responsibility bore down on her slender shoulders, and she felt the sting of helplessness.

A sudden, forceful knock rattled the wooden door, the sound reverberating through the apartment.

"Maria! Open up! Wi know seh yuh inside!" Mr. Riley's gruff voice boomed, each word soaked in impatience.

Maria's breath caught. Her hands trembled as she pulled the curtain shut, fingertips brushing against the frayed fabric. She glanced over at Marcus, trying to mask her fear with a strained smile.

"Marcus, go hide unda yuh bed, now," she whispered urgently.

"Ma, who dat?" he asked, wide-eyed.

"Just do as mi seh, please," she urged, her voice barely steady.

He hesitated, but the worry etched on his mother's face propelled him into action. Sliding off the chair, he darted toward his small bedroom, the worn floorboards creaking beneath his feet.

Another knock, more insistent this time. "Maria! If yuh nuh open di door, mi a go mek tings difficult fi yuh!"

Under his bed, Marcus curled into a tight ball, the scent of dust and old wood filling his nostrils. His heart raced, matching the rhythm of the rain that had begun tapping softly against the tin roof. He squeezed his eyes shut, willing himself to be invisible.

Maria smoothed her dress with shaking hands, her palms damp with sweat. She considered her options fleetingly—running, begging, hiding—but she knew there was no escape. Drawing a shaky breath, she moved toward the door, her footsteps echoing loudly in the suffocating silence.

Her hand hovered over the doorknob. For a moment, she stared at the peeling paint, noticing a crack that resembled a lightning bolt. *Fitting*, she thought bitterly.

"God, give mi strength," she murmured.

She turned the knob slowly, pulling the door open just a fraction. Mr. Riley's stern face loomed in the dim hallway light, his eyes narrowing as they met hers.

"Evening, Mr. Riley," she managed, her voice barely above a whisper.

"Evening? Woman, yuh know why mi deh yah," he snapped.

"Please, mi jus' need likkle more time. Mi haffi get di money together," Maria implored, her gaze dropping to the scuffed floor.

"Time? Yuh rent overdue by two weeks! Mi cyaan wait forever," he retorted, his tone sharp like shattered glass.

"Mi beg yuh, Mr. Riley. Just till di end of di week. Mi get paid Friday," she pleaded, her voice cracking.

He sighed heavily, rubbing a hand over his stubbled chin. "Three days, Maria. If mi nuh see di money by den, yuh and di boy have fi find somewhere else."

Her shoulders sagged with a mix of relief and despair. "Thank yuh," she whispered.

"Don't mek mi regret dis," he warned before turning on his heel, his footsteps fading down the corridor.

Maria closed the door softly, the latch clicking into place sounding louder than it should. She leaned her forehead against the cool wood, eyes clenched shut as a solitary tear traced a path down her cheek. The walls seemed to close in around her, the weight of their predicament pressing in from all sides.

Maria's Internal Struggle

She pressed a trembling hand to her chest, feeling the rapid thump of her heart. *How did it come to dis?* Memories of better times flickered through her mind—Marcus's laughter filling the rooms, the scent of freshly baked bread, evenings spent under the stars. Those moments felt like a lifetime ago.

"Mama?" a small voice called softly.

She turned to see Marcus standing a few feet away, his eyes shining with concern.

"Everything alright?" he asked.

She mustered a smile that didn't reach her eyes. "Of course, baby. Everything is fine."

But the façade crumbled quickly. Her legs gave way, and she sank to the floor, tears spilling freely.

"Mama!" Marcus rushed to her side.

She gathered him into her arms, holding him tightly. "Mi so sorry, Marcus. Mi trying mi best," she whispered into his hair.

He hugged her back just as fiercely. "It's okay, Mama. Mi here wid yuh."

In that embrace, surrounded by the fragile walls of their home, Maria allowed herself a moment of vulnerability. But she knew she had to be strong—for both of them.

Marcus's Silent Vow

Later that night, Marcus lay awake on his thin mattress, staring at the cracks in the ceiling that formed patterns only he could decipher. The muffled sounds of the city drifted through the open window—distant car horns, snippets of laughter, the occasional siren. But beneath it all was the lingering echo of his mother's suppressed sobs.

He clenched his fists tightly, nails digging into his palms. A fiery determination ignited within him. *One day, mi nah go mek we live like dis. Mi haffi find a way fi change tings.*

The shadows seemed to shift, and for a moment, he imagined the lines on the ceiling transforming into roads—pathways leading to a future he vowed to seize.

Bridge to Chapter 2: Transforming Thoughts into Power

As dawn approached, casting a pale glow over the city skyline, Marcus stood by the window, watching as the world slowly awakened. The chatter of early birds and the distant hum of morning traffic signaled a new day—a new opportunity.

Selene joined him, wrapping a light shawl around her shoulders. "Ready fi what's next?" she asked softly.

He turned to her, a determined glint in his eyes. "More than ever. It's time fi change di way wi think, di way wi act."

She nodded. "Mindset is everything. Let's learn, grow, and build di future wi want."

He smiled, a genuine expression of hope blossoming. "Together."

Hand in hand, they stood at the precipice of a journey that would challenge them, change them, and ultimately, empower them.

Chapter 2: Financial Mindset— Transforming Thoughts into Power

A Chance Encounter

The sun hung low in the Kingston sky, casting a warm golden hue over the bustling streets. Marcus weaved through the throng of people, the hum of lively conversation and the distant rhythm of reggae music filling the air. The scent of jerk chicken grilling mixed with the salty breeze from the harbor, creating a uniquely Jamaican aroma.

His mind raced with thoughts from the previous night—the resolve he and Selene shared to change their financial destiny. Determination fueled his steps, but uncertainty gnawed at him. *Where do I even start?* he wondered.

"Marcus? Is dat you?" a familiar voice called out.

He turned to see Daniel approaching, dressed in a crisp suit that contrasted sharply with Marcus's grease-stained coveralls. Daniel's smile was broad, his eyes hidden behind stylish sunglasses.

"Daniel! Long time, mi brother!" Marcus exclaimed, surprised.

They embraced warmly. "Look at you, man. Still di same humble guy," Daniel teased, patting Marcus on the back.

Marcus chuckled. "And yuh looking like a big executive now. Life treating yuh good, eh?"

Daniel removed his sunglasses, his eyes reflecting a mix of pride and contentment. "Can't complain. Just closed a big deal with a foreign investor. Tings moving up."

They walked together along the sidewalk, the cacophony of the city enveloping them.

"Mi remember when we used to dream 'bout making it big," Marcus reminisced.

"Yeah, man. Difference is, mi decided to take some risks," Daniel replied, his tone both nostalgic and pointed.

Marcus felt a pang of defensiveness. "What yuh mean?"

"Just that sometimes yuh haffi step outta yuh comfort zone, yuh know? Can't keep doing di same tings and expect different results," Daniel said, glancing at Marcus's attire.

"Mi running mi own garage now," Marcus said, a hint of pride in his voice.

"Dat's good, but is it really growing? Or yuh just getting by?" Daniel probed.

The question hit harder than Marcus expected. He looked away, his jaw tightening. "Mi doing what mi can."

Daniel placed a hand on his shoulder. "No disrespect, bredren. Just speaking truth. If yuh ever want to chat 'bout leveling up, give mi a call."

He handed Marcus a sleek business card embossed with his name and contact information. "Tek care, Marcus."

As Daniel strode away, disappearing into the crowd, Marcus stood rooted to the spot, the weight of the encounter settling heavily on him. The sounds of the city faded into the background as his thoughts swirled.

"Is mi really just getting by?" he questioned himself. The doubt seeped in, but alongside it ignited a spark of determination.

Seeds of Doubt and Determination

That evening, Marcus sat on the balcony of his apartment, the cool breeze rustling the leaves of the potted plants Selene lovingly tended. The stars dotted the night sky like scattered diamonds.

Selene joined him, two steaming mugs of ginger tea in hand. "Thought yuh could use dis," she said, handing him a cup.

"Thanks," he murmured, staring out into the distance.

"Everything alright?" she asked, sensing his unease.

He sighed. "Ran into Daniel today."

"Daniel? From school days?" she recalled.

"Yeah. Him doing really well—big deals, fancy suit, di whole works."

"That's good fi him," she said cautiously, noting the conflict in Marcus's tone.

"He implied that mi not pushing hard enough. That mi settling," Marcus admitted.

Selene sipped her tea thoughtfully. "Do yuh think he's right?"

"Maybe. Mi feel like mi spinning wheels, going nowhere fast," he confessed.

She took his hand gently. "Marcus, comparing yuh journey to someone else's will only rob yuh of joy. But if yuh feel like yuh can do more, den let's make a plan."

He looked into her eyes, finding comfort and resolve. "Yuh always know how fi ground me."

She smiled. "That's what partners do. So, what's di first step?"

He leaned back, contemplating. "Mi think mi need fi change di way mi think 'bout money. Maybe mi holding miself back wid limiting beliefs."

"Den let's start dere," Selene agreed. "Mindset is di foundation fi everything."

The Mentor Appears

A few days later, Marcus visited the local library, a modest building nestled between a community center and a bustling marketplace. The scent of old books and polished wood greeted him as he stepped inside.

He perused the finance section, his fingers trailing over titles that promised wealth and success. One book caught his eye: *"Think and Grow Rich—The Caribbean Edition."*

"Good choice," a voice sounded beside him.

He turned to see an elderly man with silver-gray locks and wise eyes that seemed to hold a universe of knowledge.

"Mi sorry, didn't mean to intrude," Marcus said politely.

The man chuckled. "No intrusion at all. Name's Mr. Thompson, but folks around here call me Uncle Roy."

"Nice to meet yuh, Uncle Roy. Mi name's Marcus."

"Ah, Marcus. Yuh looking fi ways fi elevate yuh financial situation, eh?" Uncle Roy asked, his gaze penetrating yet kind.

"Trying to," Marcus admitted. "Feel like mi missing something."

Uncle Roy nodded knowingly. "Money is a funny ting. It's as much 'bout mindset as it is 'bout numbers."

"Dat's what mi starting to realize," Marcus replied.

"Tell yuh what, why don't yuh join me for a cup of tea? Mi have some stories and maybe a few lessons to share," Uncle Roy offered.

Marcus hesitated briefly but felt an inexplicable pull toward the man. "Alright, sure."

Wisdom Over Tea

They sat at a small café adjacent to the library, the aroma of freshly brewed bush tea enveloping them.

"So, Marcus, tell me 'bout yuhself," Uncle Roy prompted.

"Well, mi run a small garage. Been working hard, but tings not progressing how mi want dem to," he shared.

Uncle Roy sipped his tea thoughtfully. "And why do yuh think dat is?"

"Maybe mi don't have di right resources. Or maybe di economy tough," Marcus speculated.

"Or maybe it's how yuh thinking 'bout money and success," Uncle Roy suggested.

Marcus raised an eyebrow. "What yuh mean?"

"Let me tell yuh a story," Uncle Roy began. "Dere was a farmer who had two sons. One son believed dat hard work alone would bring success. He toiled in di fields from sunrise to sunset but barely eked out a living. Di other son studied di land, learned new techniques, and embraced new ideas. His crops flourished, and he prospered."

"What's di difference?" Marcus asked, intrigued.

"Mindset," Uncle Roy said simply. "Di first son was stuck in his ways, thinking hard work was enough. Di second son opened his mind to possibilities."

Marcus nodded slowly. "So, yuh saying mi need fi change how mi see tings."

"Exactly. If yuh always thinking small, yuh bank account will stay small," Uncle Roy smiled.

"How do mi start?" Marcus asked earnestly.

"First, identify di limiting beliefs holding yuh back. Den, replace dem with empowering ones," Uncle Roy advised.

"Sounds easier said than done," Marcus admitted.

Uncle Roy chuckled. "Change is never easy, but it's worth it. Remember, 'As a man thinketh in his heart, so is he.'"

Challenging Old Beliefs

That night, Marcus sat at his kitchen table, a blank notebook before him. Selene watched from across the room, sensing the intensity of his focus.

"What yuh working on?" she asked.

"Writing down mi beliefs 'bout money," he replied without looking up.

"Interesting. Mind if mi join yuh?" she offered.

"Please," he smiled, grateful for her support.

They began listing everything that came to mind:

- Money hard fi get.
- Rich people selfish or crooked.
- Success only come fi certain people.
- Better to play it safe than take risks.

Selene looked over the list. "No wonder we feel stuck wid beliefs like these."

He sighed. "It's what we grow up hearing. But Uncle Roy seh we need fi replace dem."

"Alright, let's flip dem," she suggested.

Together, they transformed each belief:

- Money flows easily when we provide value.
- Wealthy people can be generous and ethical.
- Success is available to anyone who pursues it.
- Taking calculated risks leads to growth.

As they finished, Marcus felt a weight lifting. "Dis feels... liberating."

She nodded. "Now, we need fi internalize dem."

He met her gaze, determination shining in his eyes. "And act on dem."

Taking the First Step

Encouraged by their breakthrough, Marcus decided to attend a local entrepreneurship seminar recommended by Uncle Roy. The event buzzed with energy, people from all walks of life eager to learn and connect.

At the entrance, a banner read: "Unlock Your Potential—Think Big, Achieve Bigger."

Inside, speakers shared stories of overcoming adversity, embracing innovation, and the power of a growth mindset.

One speaker, a charismatic woman named Jasmine Thompson, captivated the audience with her journey from a street vendor to a successful restaurant owner.

"Mi realized dat di only limits are di ones we place on ourselves," she declared passionately. "When mi stopped seeing obstacles and started seeing opportunities, everything changed."

Marcus felt her words resonate deep within. *If she can do it, so can I.*

Embracing a New Perspective

After the seminar, Marcus approached Jasmine.

"Excuse me, Miss Thompson. Mi name is Marcus. Yuh story really inspired me," he greeted nervously.

She smiled warmly. "Thank yuh, Marcus. Happy to hear dat. What do yuh do?"

"Mi run a small garage. Trying fi grow it, but mi realize mi need fi change mi mindset first," he admitted.

"That's a big realization. Most people never get dat far," she encouraged.

"Do yuh have any advice fi someone in mi position?" he asked earnestly.

"Surround yuhself with people who uplift and challenge yuh. Invest in learning and don't be afraid fi step outta yuh comfort zone," she replied.

He nodded thoughtfully. "Mi appreciate dat."

"Here," she handed him a card. "We're having a networking event next week. Come by. Mi think yuh might find it valuable."

"Definitely. Thank yuh so much," Marcus said, his spirits lifted.

Confronting Fear

Back at the garage, Marcus began implementing small changes. He reorganized the workspace, updated tools, and considered offering new services. But self-doubt lingered.

One afternoon, while wrestling with an engine that refused to cooperate, his old friend Peter dropped by.

"Yo, Marcus! Long time, mi bredda!" Peter called out.

"Peter! Wha gwaan?" Marcus wiped his hands, happy to see a familiar face.

Peter leaned against the workbench. "Ah, yuh know me. Same old, same old. Heard yuh running dis place now."

"Yeah, trying fi take it to di next level," Marcus said.

Peter smirked. "Careful, man. Ambition can lead to disappointment. Mi uncle tried expanding his business and lost everything."

Marcus felt a pang of irritation. "People succeed every day."

"True, but not everyone. Sometimes it's better fi stick with what yuh know," Peter cautioned.

"Is dis mi fear talking through him?" Marcus wondered.

He straightened up. "Appreciate di concern, but mi not letting fear hold me back."

Peter shrugged. "Just saying. Anyway, good luck."

As Peter left, Marcus felt reaffirmed in his decision. *Fear won't dictate mi choices.*

A Symbolic Lesson

Later that week, Marcus met with Uncle Roy at a riverside park. Children played nearby, their laughter mingling with the gentle rush of the water.

"How tings progressing?" Uncle Roy asked.

"Making strides, but sometimes mi feel doubt creeping in," Marcus confessed.

Uncle Roy picked up two stones from the riverbank. "See these? One is smooth, di other rough. Di smooth one has been in di water a long time, shaped by persistence. Di rough one is untouched, unchanged."

He handed Marcus the stones. "Which one do yuh want to be?"

Marcus turned them over in his hands. "Di smooth one. Shaped by experiences."

"Exactly. Yuh have to let life's currents shape yuh. Can't remain unchanged and expect growth," Uncle Roy smiled.

"Yuh always have a way wid metaphors," Marcus laughed.

"Comes with age," Uncle Roy winked. "Remember, 'The longest journey starts with a single step.' Keep moving forward."

Building a Support Network

At Jasmine's networking event, Marcus found himself among entrepreneurs, creatives, and professionals—all buzzing with ideas and ambition.

He struck up conversations, exchanging stories and insights. The initial nerves faded as he realized everyone was there to grow and support each other.

One attendee, a graphic designer named Raj, offered his services to revamp Marcus's business branding.

"First impressions matter, boss," Raj insisted. "Let's give yuh garage a fresh look."

"Di way people see yuh business can change how dey feel 'bout it," Marcus agreed.

They exchanged contact information, and Marcus felt a surge of excitement. *This is what Uncle Roy and Jasmine were talking about.*

Facing the Ultimate Test

Despite the positive momentum, a significant challenge loomed. The landlord of the building housing Marcus's garage informed him of a substantial rent increase.

"Yuh kidding me? An increase of dis size will cripple mi business!" Marcus exclaimed.

"Sorry, but mi have mi own expenses. If yuh can't pay, I'll have to find someone who can," the landlord said unapologetically.

Panic threatened to overtake him, but Marcus took a deep breath. *Stay calm. Think.*

He reached out to Uncle Roy and Jasmine for advice.

"Maybe dis is an opportunity in disguise," Jasmine suggested over the phone.

"How so?" Marcus asked.

"Could be time fi relocate to a better area or even buy yuh own space," she proposed.

"Buy mi own? Mi nuh have dat kind of money," he protested.

"With the right plan and maybe a business loan, it's possible. Remember, think big," she encouraged.

Uncle Roy echoed similar sentiments. "Sometimes di universe pushes us so we can spread our wings."

A Leap of Faith

Determined, Marcus began researching properties and exploring financing options. He put together a business plan, highlighting his vision for the garage's expansion.

At the bank, the loan officer, Ms. Williams, reviewed his proposal.

"Impressive plan, Mr. Thomas. But do yuh have any collateral?" she inquired.

"Not much, but mi have a solid customer base and projections showing growth," he replied.

She considered for a moment. "Normally, we'd require more assets, but we do have a program supporting local small businesses. It's risky, but mi believe in investing in our community."

Relief washed over him. "Thank yuh so much. Yuh won't regret it."

Victory and Validation

With the loan approved, Marcus secured a new location—a larger space in a more visible area. Raj helped design a fresh logo and signage, giving the garage a modern appeal.

At the grand reopening, customers old and new gathered. Selene stood by his side, pride shining in her eyes.

"Look at what yuh accomplished," she whispered.

"Couldn't have done it without yuh," he replied, squeezing her hand.

Uncle Roy and Jasmine approached, congratulatory smiles on their faces.

"See what happens when yuh shift yuh mindset?" Jasmine remarked.

"Di sky is truly di limit," Marcus agreed.

Wisdom

As the celebration continued, Uncle Roy raised a toast.

"To Marcus, who learned dat 'If yuh nuh step out di boat, yuh can't walk pon water.' May dis be just di beginning."

Laughter and cheers followed, the warmth of community enveloping them all.

Bridge to Chapter 3: Embracing Discipline

Later that night, amidst the joy, Marcus knew this was just the first step.

"Now comes di hard part—maintaining and growing dis success," he mused to Selene.

"True. It will require discipline and smart management," she responded.

He nodded. "Time fi turn thoughts into consistent action."

She smiled. "And mi wi be right here to keep yuh accountable."

In the next chapter, Marcus delves into the practices that sustain growth. He learns that a shifted mindset must be paired with discipline to truly transform his financial reality.

Financial Lessons Woven into the Story

1. **Mindset Shapes Reality**
    a. Limiting beliefs can hinder progress. By identifying and replacing them, Marcus opens himself to new opportunities.
2. **The Power of Mentorship**
    a. Guidance from Uncle Roy and inspiration from Jasmine highlight the importance of learning from others' experiences.
3. **Networking and Relationships**
    a. Building connections expands resources, support, and opens doors that would remain closed otherwise.
4. **Embracing Risks**
    a. Calculated risks, like relocating his garage, lead to significant growth.
5. **Overcoming Fear**
    a. Recognizing fear as a barrier allows Marcus to push past it and pursue his goals.

Interactive Element: Reflecting on Your Mindset

Exercise: Identify and Transform Limiting Beliefs

- **List Your Current Beliefs About Money**

- What do you believe about wealth, success, and your ability to achieve them?
- **Challenge Each Belief**
    - Is this belief based on fact or perception?
- **Replace with Empowering Beliefs**
    - Transform negative statements into positive affirmations.
- **Action Plan**
    - What steps can you take to internalize these new beliefs?

Thoughts

Marcus's journey in transforming his mindset illustrates that true change begins within. By challenging his beliefs, seeking guidance, and embracing new perspectives, he sets the foundation for lasting success.

Chapter 3: Embracing Financial Discipline—Turning Thoughts into Actions

The First Financial Test

The morning sun cast a warm glow over Marcus's newly expanded garage. The fresh paint gleamed, and the crisp logo designed by Raj stood proudly above the entrance. The hum of vehicles and the rhythmic clinking of tools created a symphony that filled him with pride. Business was picking up, and for the first time in a long while, Marcus felt the winds of change blowing in his favor.

But as the day progressed, clouds gathered—both in the sky and in his circumstances.

"Boss, we have a problem," Junior, one of his mechanics, approached with a concerned expression.

"What's up?" Marcus asked, wiping his hands on a rag.

"The hydraulic lift is acting up again. It's not safe to use until we get it fixed."

Marcus frowned. "Didn't we just service dat equipment?"

Junior nodded. "Yeah, but di technician said it was a temporary fix. We need a full replacement."

Marcus rubbed his temples. "How much we talking?"

"About a hundred and fifty thousand Jamaican dollars," Junior replied apologetically.

Marcus's heart sank. That was a significant hit to their finances. "Alright, thanks for letting me know. Let's see how we can work around it for now."

As Junior returned to work, Selene arrived, carrying a bag of lunch for Marcus. "Hey, thought you could use a break," she said with a smile.

He forced a grin. "Yuh timing is perfect as always."

They sat in his small office, the aroma of jerk chicken filling the space. Marcus poked at his food, his mind elsewhere.

"What's bothering you?" Selene asked, her eyes searching his.

He sighed. "Di hydraulic lift needs replacing. It's a big expense we didn't plan for."

She nodded thoughtfully. "That's tough. Do we have enough in di budget to cover it?"

Marcus hesitated. "Not exactly. Wi have some money set aside, but with di supplier increasing prices and other expenses, tings tight."

Selene reached out and held his hand. "We'll figure it out. Remember, this is just a hurdle, not a roadblock."

Just then, his phone buzzed. A message from his parts supplier: *"Urgent notice: Due to rising costs, prices will increase by 15% effective immediately."*

Marcus's grip tightened on the phone. "Yuh must be kidding me!"

Selene leaned over to read the message. "Another price increase?"

"Dis is too much. Between di equipment and dis, mi nuh know how we going manage," he said, frustration creeping into his voice.

"Maybe we can find a way to adjust di budget or negotiate with di supplier?" she suggested.

He shook his head. "Mi tried. Dey seh dere's nothing dey can do. Everything piling up at once."

Selene squeezed his hand gently. "Marcus, we can get through this. Let's look at di finances together and see where we can make adjustments."

He nodded reluctantly. "Alright. Let's tackle it head-on."

Uncle Roy's Financial Discipline Lesson

Later that afternoon, Marcus decided to seek counsel from Uncle Roy. He found him sitting under a large mango tree near the community center, watching a group of children play soccer.

"Uncle Roy, mi need fi talk," Marcus said as he approached.

Uncle Roy looked up with a welcoming smile. "Ah, Marcus. Have a seat, young man. What's on your mind?"

Marcus sat beside him, the shade providing a respite from the heat. "Everything seems to be going wrong at di garage. Equipment failure, supplier price hikes—mi feel like tings falling apart."

Uncle Roy nodded thoughtfully. "Challenges are a part of any journey. How yuh planning to handle dem?"

"That's di problem. Mi nuh sure. Mi feel like mi losing control," Marcus admitted.

Uncle Roy picked up a fallen mango, examining it. "Marcus, yuh ever plant yam before?"

Marcus gave him a puzzled look. "No, Uncle Roy. Mi not much of a farmer."

He chuckled. "Let me tell yuh something about farming. When yuh plant yam, it takes nine months before yuh can harvest. During dat time, yuh haffi tend to it—water it, keep di weeds away, protect it from pests. Yuh can't rush it, and yuh can't neglect it."

"Okay, but how dat relate to mi situation?" Marcus asked.

"Business is like planting yam. Yuh have to be patient and plan ahead. Unexpected tings will happen—droughts, storms—but if yuh prepare yourself, yuh can handle dem without losing di whole crop," Uncle Roy explained.

"So yuh saying mi need fi plan fi di unexpected? Like having savings set aside?" Marcus inferred.

"Exactly. Cash flow is di lifeblood of yuh business. Without proper management, even a small problem can become a big disaster," Uncle Roy said, his eyes steady on Marcus.

Marcus sighed. "Mi thought expanding di garage would solve mi problems, but it seem to bring more."

"Growth brings new challenges. That's why financial discipline is crucial. Do yuh have a budget?"

"Not a detailed one. Mi just keep track of expenses in mi head mostly," Marcus admitted sheepishly.

Uncle Roy shook his head gently. "Dat won't do, Marcus. Yuh need to see exactly where every dollar is coming and going. 'If yuh fail to plan, yuh plan to fail.'"

Marcus nodded slowly. "Mi understand. Mi need fi get serious about mi finances."

"Glad to hear it. And remember, always set aside something for emergencies. Dat way, when di unexpected happens, yuh not caught off guard," Uncle Roy advised.

"Thank yuh, Uncle Roy. Yuh always have di right words," Marcus said appreciatively.

"Anytime, son. Now go and take control of yuh ship before it sails off course," Uncle Roy encouraged.

The Budgeting Breakdown

That evening, Marcus and Selene sat at their kitchen table, papers spread out before them. Receipts, invoices, and notebooks created a mosaic of their financial reality.

"Alright, let's start with all di income," Selene suggested, pen in hand.

Marcus nodded. "From di garage, we bringing in about three hundred thousand Jamaican dollars per month."

Selene wrote it down. "Okay. Now, let's list out all di expenses."

They went through each item meticulously:

- **Rent for Garage:** 80,000 JMD
- **Staff Salaries:** 100,000 JMD
- **Utilities (Electricity, Water):** 20,000 JMD
- **Supplies and Parts:** 50,000 JMD
- **Loan Payments:** 30,000 JMD
- **Miscellaneous Expenses:** 15,000 JMD

As they totaled the expenses, Marcus felt the weight of reality pressing on him. "Dat's 295,000 JMD in expenses."

"Which leaves us with only 5,000 JMD surplus each month," Selene noted, concern evident.

"That can't be right. Where all di money going?" Marcus asked, eyebrows furrowed.

Selene tapped the pen thoughtfully. "Let's look at di miscellaneous expenses."

They dove deeper, uncovering small but frequent costs:

- **Daily Lunches Ordered:** 15,000 JMD per month
- **Unplanned Purchases:** 10,000 JMD per month
- **Personal Withdrawals:** 5,000 JMD per month

Marcus ran a hand over his face. "Mi never realize how much di small tings add up."

"Every mickle mek a muckle," Selene reminded him gently. "If we cut back on unnecessary spending, we can free up funds."

"Yuh right. We can start by preparing lunch at home and cutting down on personal spending," he agreed.

Selene smiled. "Exactly. Also, we should set up an emergency fund."

"With what money?" Marcus asked skeptically.

"By reallocating di savings from reduced expenses. Even if it's just 20,000 JMD a month, it's a start," she suggested.

"Alright, let's do it. Mi see now how important dis is," Marcus conceded.

They continued working late into the night, creating a detailed budget and setting financial goals.

Interactive Moment: Marcus's Monthly Budget

Income:

- **Garage Revenue:** 300,000 JMD

Expenses:

- **Rent:** 80,000 JMD
- **Staff Salaries:** 100,000 JMD
- **Utilities:** 20,000 JMD
- **Supplies:** 50,000 JMD
- **Loan Payments:** 30,000 JMD
- **Miscellaneous (Reduced):** 10,000 JMD
- **Emergency Fund Contribution:** 20,000 JMD

Total Expenses: 310,000 JMD

Adjusted Net Income: -10,000 JMD

Adjustments Made:

- Reduced miscellaneous expenses by 20,000 JMD
- Introduced emergency fund contribution
- Identified need to increase income or further reduce expenses

"Wait, we still in di negative," Marcus observed, concern returning.

Selene nodded. "Then we need to find ways to increase revenue or make additional cuts."

"Maybe we can offer new services or promote di business more aggressively," he suggested.

"That's a good idea. Also, consider renegotiating with suppliers or finding more affordable options," Selene added.

"Mi will look into dat first ting tomorrow," Marcus affirmed.

An Unexpected Temptation

The next day, as Marcus was locking up the garage, his old friend Desmond pulled up in a shiny new car.

"Marcus! Long time no see, mi brethren!" Desmond called out, stepping out with a wide grin.

"Desmond! Wha gwaan?" Marcus greeted him with a handshake.

"Man, tings looking up fi me. Just got into a new business venture," Desmond boasted.

"Nice ride," Marcus commented, eyeing the car.

"Thanks. And dat's what mi came to talk to yuh about. There's an investment opportunity yuh might be interested in," Desmond said, his tone conspiratorial.

Marcus raised an eyebrow. "Oh yeah? Tell me more."

"There's dis new cryptocurrency that's about to blow up. Mi have insider info dat it's going to triple in value within di next month," Desmond explained excitedly.

"Crypto-what? Mi nuh know 'bout dat kinda ting," Marcus said cautiously.

"Trust me, man. Mi already mek a big profit, and mi wanted to share di opportunity wid yuh. All yuh need is a minimum of 200,000 JMD to start," Desmond urged.

Marcus felt a rush of temptation. The potential profits could solve his financial issues quickly. "Mi nuh have dat kinda cash lying around."

"Come on, Marcus. Dis could change yuh life. Don't let dis chance pass yuh by," Desmond pressed.

"I'll think about it," Marcus replied, his mind racing.

"Don't take too long, opportunities like dis don't wait," Desmond warned before driving off.

That evening, Marcus wrestled with the decision. The allure of quick money was strong.

"Selene, Desmond came by today with an investment opportunity," he began hesitantly.

She looked up from her book. "What kind of opportunity?"

"He talking 'bout some new cryptocurrency. Claims it will triple in value soon," Marcus explained.

Selene frowned. "Sounds risky. Do yuh know much about it?"

"Not really, but Desmond seems confident," he admitted.

"Marcus, yuh just started getting our finances in order. Is it wise to risk our money on something so uncertain?" she cautioned.

"But if it pays off, it could solve our problems," he argued.

"Or it could make dem worse. Remember, 'All that glitters is not gold,'" she said firmly.

He sighed. "Maybe yuh right. Mi just tired of struggling."

"Quick money often comes with big risks. Let's stick to our plan," Selene insisted.

Marcus nodded slowly. "Alright. We'll stay the course."

The Moment of Growth

The following day, Desmond called. "So, yuh ready to invest?" he asked eagerly.

"Mi thought about it, Desmond, but mi going to pass," Marcus replied.

"Really? Mi trying to help yuh out here," Desmond pressed.

"I appreciate it, but mi haffi be smart with mi money right now," Marcus stated confidently.

Desmond scoffed. "Suit yourself. Don't say I didn't warn yuh when yuh see mi rolling in cash."

"All di best to yuh," Marcus said before hanging up.

A sense of relief washed over him. He knew he'd made the right choice.

Later that week, an unexpected opportunity arose. A local delivery company needed a reliable mechanic for their fleet and approached Marcus with a contract.

"Wi heard good tings about yuh garage," the manager explained. "We're looking for someone to handle regular maintenance on ten vehicles."

"That sounds great!" Marcus responded enthusiastically. "Let's discuss the terms."

The contract promised steady work and income, significantly boosting the garage's revenue.

When he shared the news with Selene, she beamed. "See what happens when yuh stay focused and disciplined?"

He grinned. "Yuh were right. Patience pays off."

Cliffhanger

Just as things seemed to be falling into place, Marcus received a letter in the mail. Opening it, his eyes widened in disbelief.

"Notice of Zoning Regulation Changes Affecting Your Business."

He read on anxiously. The city planned to implement new regulations that could potentially impact the operation of his garage.

Selene noticed his distress. "What's wrong?"

"Looks like we have another challenge ahead," Marcus said, handing her the letter.

She scanned the document. "This could complicate things."

He took a deep breath. "Well, we overcame obstacles before. We'll figure this out too."

Key Financial Lessons Woven into the Story

1. **Financial Discipline Equals Freedom**
   a. Marcus learns that managing his money wisely allows him to navigate unexpected expenses without derailing his business.
2. **Budgeting Equals Awareness and Control**
   a. By creating a detailed budget, Marcus gains insight into his financial situation, enabling him to make informed decisions.
3. **Emergency Funds Equal Security**
   a. Understanding the importance of setting aside funds for unforeseen events helps Marcus prepare for and handle crises.
4. **Patience vs. Quick Money**
   a. Marcus resists the temptation of a risky investment, choosing long-term stability over the allure of fast cash.
5. **Consistency Over Hustle Mentality**
   a. Committing to his financial plan and maintaining discipline leads to sustainable growth for Marcus's business.

Thoughts

Marcus's journey continues as he transforms his newfound mindset into tangible actions. By embracing financial discipline, he takes control of his destiny, learning that success isn't just about big leaps but consistent, measured steps.

Will Marcus overcome the new regulatory challenges threatening his business? Can he maintain his disciplined approach in the face of mounting pressures?

Find out in the next chapter as Marcus navigates the complexities of business growth and resilience.

Chapter 4: Navigating Growth and Overcoming Bureaucracy

The Regulatory Bombshell

The morning sun bathed the garage in a warm glow, reflecting off the freshly polished cars lined up outside. Marcus felt a surge of pride as he surveyed his bustling business. Customers chatted animatedly, and the steady rhythm of tools echoed from the workshop. It seemed like everything was finally falling into place.

As he sorted through the day's mail, one envelope caught his eye. It was official-looking, stamped with the emblem of the Kingston Municipal Council. Frowning slightly, he tore it open.

"Notice of Zoning Regulation Changes Affecting Your Business."

Marcus's heart skipped a beat. He scanned the letter, but the dense legal jargon made his head spin.

"Due to amendments in municipal zoning laws, businesses operating within specified residential zones are required to comply with new regulations pertaining to environmental impact, building codes, and commercial operations..."

"What di...?" he muttered under his breath.

Just then, Selene walked in, carrying a tray with two cups of steaming coffee.

"Hey love, thought you might need a pick-me-up," she said cheerfully.

He looked up, worry etched across his face. "Selene, yuh need fi see dis."

He handed her the letter. She read through it carefully, her brow furrowing.

"What does all this mean?" she asked.

"From what mi can tell, dem changing di zoning laws, and it might affect di garage. Mi nuh sure if mi can even operate here anymore," he said, frustration creeping into his voice.

"Easy, Marcus. Let's not jump to conclusions. It might not be as bad as it seems," Selene soothed.

"Mi cyaan afford fi shut down! Dis place is everything," he exclaimed.

"Maybe we should talk to someone who understands these things. Uncle Roy might have some advice, or we could consult a professional," she suggested.

He sighed deeply. "Yuh right. Mi just feel like every time tings start go good, someting come fi knock mi down."

Selene placed a reassuring hand on his shoulder. "We'll figure it out together. Remember, 'Trouble nuh set like rain,' but we can prepare fi it."

He managed a small smile. "Thanks, Selene. Let's see what Uncle Roy has to say."

Seeking Legal and Business Advice

Later that afternoon, Marcus and Selene sat across from Uncle Roy on his veranda. The scent of blooming hibiscus filled the air, and the distant sound of children playing added a backdrop of normalcy to an otherwise stressful situation.

Uncle Roy adjusted his glasses as he reviewed the letter. "Hmm, dis is a bit complex, but it nuh necessarily mean di end of di road."

"Uncle Roy, mi cyaan even understand half of what dem saying," Marcus admitted.

He nodded thoughtfully. "Bureaucracy love fi wrap tings up in fancy words. But knowledge is power. Mi know a man who specializes in dis kinda ting. Mr. Edwards—smart as a whip when it comes to business law and regulations."

"Mi nuh have money fi pay lawyer fees right now," Marcus said, worry evident in his tone.

Uncle Roy waved a dismissive hand. "Don't fret 'bout dat. Mr. Edwards does consultations for small businesses at a reasonable rate. Him more interested in helping di community than making a quick buck."

Selene chimed in, "It wouldn't hurt to at least hear what he has to say."

Marcus took a deep breath. "Alright, let's set it up."

The next day, they met Mr. Edwards at his modest office downtown. The walls were lined with bookshelves, filled to the brim with legal tomes and binders.

Mr. Edwards greeted them warmly. "Good afternoon. You must be Marcus and Selene. Please, have a seat."

"Thanks for seeing us on such short notice," Marcus said appreciatively.

"Of course. Uncle Roy speaks highly of you," Mr. Edwards replied.

He reviewed the letter carefully, his eyes scanning each line with practiced ease.

"Well, the good news is they're not shutting you down," Mr. Edwards began.

Marcus exhaled, relief washing over him. "Thank God."

"However," Mr. Edwards continued, "they are requiring you to make certain upgrades to comply with new environmental and safety regulations."

"Upgrades? Like what?" Marcus asked.

"According to this, you'll need to install a proper drainage system to prevent oil and chemical runoff, improve waste disposal methods, and make adjustments to your building to meet updated codes," Mr. Edwards explained.

Selene glanced at Marcus. "That sounds expensive."

Mr. Edwards nodded. "It can be, but there are options. You could consider applying for a small business grant or loan to cover the costs. Alternatively, you can petition for an extension or negotiate the terms."

Marcus rubbed his temples. "Mi just expanded di business. Funds tight right now. And mi nuh have time fi run around dealing with di government."

Mr. Edwards leaned forward. "I understand it's overwhelming, but navigating these regulations is part of growing a business. With the right approach, this can become an opportunity rather than just an obstacle."

"What do you suggest?" Marcus asked.

"First, let's respond to this notice formally, acknowledging their requirements and requesting a meeting to discuss practical timelines. Then, we can explore financial assistance programs that you may qualify for," Mr. Edwards outlined.

Selene touched Marcus's arm gently. "See? It's manageable. We're not alone in this."

Marcus took a deep breath. "Alright, let's do it. Thank you, Mr. Edwards."

"Happy to help. Remember, 'Every setback is a setup for a comeback,'" Mr. Edwards smiled.

The Crossroads – Risk vs. Reward

Back at home, Marcus sat at the kitchen table, staring at a list of options they'd compiled.

Selene joined him, placing a cup of tea by his side. "Penny for your thoughts?"

"Mi trying fi figure out di best path forward. Do mi comply with di regulations and spend money mi nuh really have? Do mi fight it and risk making tings worse? Or do mi try fi relocate?" Marcus mused aloud.

"Relocating could be an opportunity to find a better location," Selene suggested.

"True, but moving di garage would be expensive and disruptive. We might lose customers during di transition," he countered.

Just then, his phone rang. It was Jasmine.

"Hey Marcus! Uncle Roy told me what's going on. How are you holding up?" she asked, concern in her voice.

"Mi hanging in there. Just trying fi decide mi next move," he replied.

"Well, sometimes when life gives you lemons, you make lemonade. Have you thought about turning this challenge into a chance to expand even more?" Jasmine proposed.

"Funny enough, Selene and I were discussing dat," Marcus said, glancing at Selene.

"Listen, I have some contacts who could help you find potential investors or grants. There's a program supporting small businesses in our area looking to grow sustainably," Jasmine offered.

"That would be amazing. Mi appreciate any help," Marcus said gratefully.

"Great! Let's meet tomorrow and brainstorm," Jasmine suggested.

After hanging up, Marcus felt a glimmer of hope.

Later that evening, Uncle Roy stopped by.

"Afternoon, you two. How goes di battle plan?" he asked.

"Weighing mi options. Jasmine thinks we should use dis as an opportunity to level up," Marcus explained.

Uncle Roy nodded approvingly. "She's a smart woman. Sometimes progress requires stepping out of di comfort zone."

"But what if it doesn't work out? Mi nuh want fi risk everything and end up with nothing," Marcus expressed his fears.

"Marcus, 'He who fears failure limits his activities.' Success is not final, failure is not fatal. It's di courage to continue that counts," Uncle Roy counseled.

Selene smiled softly. "We believe in you, Marcus. Whatever decision you make, we're behind you."

He looked between them, the weight of their support bolstering his resolve. "Alright. Let's explore every option before making a choice."

Business Expansion and Investment Strategy

The next day, Marcus met with Jasmine at a local café bustling with energy. The aroma of freshly brewed Blue Mountain coffee filled the air.

"Glad you could make it," Jasmine greeted him with a warm hug.

"Thanks for meeting me," Marcus responded.

They sat down, and Jasmine pulled out her tablet. "Okay, so I did some digging. There's a government grant aimed at businesses looking to improve environmental compliance and expand sustainably."

"Really? Dat sounds perfect," Marcus said, intrigued.

"Yes! It can cover up to 70% of your upgrade costs. Plus, I know an investor interested in supporting local entrepreneurs who have a solid plan," she explained.

"What's di catch?" he asked cautiously.

"No catch, but you need a comprehensive business proposal outlining how you'll not only comply with regulations but also how you plan to grow and contribute to the community," Jasmine clarified.

Marcus nodded thoughtfully. "Mi can do dat. Mi have ideas for expanding services and maybe even training programs for young mechanics."

"That's exactly the kind of initiative they love to support," Jasmine encouraged.

Feeling energized, Marcus spent the next few days crafting his proposal. He outlined plans for:

- Upgrading the garage to meet and exceed environmental standards.
- Expanding services to include eco-friendly vehicle options.
- Creating apprenticeship programs for local youth.

He also scouted a nearby vacant lot that was larger and better suited for his expanded vision. It was a bold move, but one that could secure the future of his business.

Sitting in Mr. Edwards's office, they reviewed the proposal.

"This is impressive, Marcus. With this, you have a strong chance of securing both the grant and investor support," Mr. Edwards remarked.

"Thank you. I couldn't have done it without everyone's help," Marcus said humbly.

"Now, we need to prepare for the presentation to the grant committee and meetings with potential investors," Mr. Edwards advised.

"Mi ready fi it," Marcus asserted confidently.

The Unexpected Opposition

Just as things seemed to be aligning, word began to spread about Marcus's ambitious plans. Not everyone was pleased.

One afternoon, as Marcus was leaving the garage, a man approached him. He was tall, with a stern expression and a sharp suit.

"You're Marcus Thomas, right?" the man asked.

"Yes. Can I help you?" Marcus replied cautiously.

"Name's Mr. Hutchinson. I own Hutchinson's Auto Repairs down di road," he stated.

Marcus extended his hand. "Nice to meet you."

Mr. Hutchinson ignored the gesture. "I've heard about your plans to expand. Impressive, but I hope you're aware that this area can't support too many big garages."

Marcus frowned slightly. "Kingston is growing. There's room for all of us."

Mr. Hutchinson smirked. "Perhaps, but just so you know, I have connections on the zoning board. It would be a shame if your application ran into... complications."

"Are you threatening me?" Marcus asked, keeping his tone even.

"Just giving you a friendly heads-up. Sometimes it's better to know your place than to overextend," Mr. Hutchinson warned before walking away.

Marcus felt a surge of anger and concern. *So this is how it's going to be?*

He immediately called Mr. Edwards to relay the encounter.

"This is unfortunate but not entirely surprising," Mr. Edwards said. "Competition can sometimes lead to underhanded tactics."

"Can he really influence di zoning board against me?" Marcus asked.

"It's possible, but there are ways to counteract that. We can ensure your application is solid and perhaps gather community support to back your proposal," Mr. Edwards suggested.

That evening, Marcus met with Selene, Uncle Roy, and Jasmine to discuss the new threat.

"That man has some nerve," Selene said indignantly.

"Well, 'Dog nyam him supper' if he thinks he can bully you," Uncle Roy declared.

"Perhaps we can turn this to our advantage," Jasmine mused.

"How so?" Marcus inquired.

"Let's build a coalition of community members who support your business. Testimonials, endorsements—showing that your garage is an asset to the area," she elaborated.

"That's a great idea," Selene agreed. "We'll show them that we're here to uplift, not disrupt."

Marcus nodded. "Alright. Let's rally di community."

Over the next few weeks, Marcus and his team worked tirelessly. They attended neighborhood meetings, shared his vision, and gathered signatures for a petition supporting his expansion.

The local press caught wind of the story, featuring articles about a hometown entrepreneur striving to make a positive impact.

However, just when momentum was building, Mr. Edwards delivered troubling news.

"Marcus, I've just been informed that the zoning board has added new requirements to your application," he said grimly.

"New requirements? Like what?" Marcus asked.

"An environmental impact study, which could take months and cost a significant amount," Mr. Edwards explained.

"Unbelievable! Dis is Hutchinson's doing, mi sure of it," Marcus exclaimed.

"Possibly, but we need to address it strategically," Mr. Edwards advised.

Cliffhanger

Marcus stood at the crossroads once again, facing a daunting obstacle that threatened to derail everything he had worked for.

"Mi feel like every step forward pulls mi two steps back," he confided to Selene.

She took his hand, her eyes determined. "We didn't come this far to give up now. We'll find a way."

He gazed into the distance, the city lights flickering like embers. "Then that's exactly what we'll do. Mi not backing down."

Key Financial Lessons Woven into the Story

1. **Navigating Bureaucracy is a Business Skill**
   a. Marcus learns the importance of understanding laws and regulations to protect and advance his business.
2. **Think Expansion, Not Just Survival**

a. Instead of simply reacting to challenges, Marcus uses them as opportunities to grow strategically.
3. **The Power of Networking and Advocacy**
    a. Building relationships with community members, professionals, and peers strengthens his position.
4. **Strategic Investment vs. Emotional Decisions**
    a. Marcus makes calculated choices, seeking advice and exploring all options rather than acting impulsively.
5. **Resilience in the Face of Competition**
    a. Facing sabotage and unfair tactics, Marcus remains steadfast, demonstrating perseverance.

Thoughts

Marcus's journey through the complexities of business growth highlights the challenges many entrepreneurs face. Bureaucracy and competition can be formidable obstacles, but with knowledge, community support, and strategic planning, they can be overcome.

Will Marcus find a way to meet the new requirements and secure his business's future? Can he outmaneuver those who wish to see him fail?

Join us in the next chapter as Marcus battles the odds, learning that true success often requires not just ambition and discipline, but also resilience and unity.

Chapter 5: Overcoming Opposition and Securing His Future

The Pressure Intensifies

The afternoon sun cast long shadows across Marcus's garage as he stood outside, staring at the official letter trembling in his hands. The zoning board had sent another notice—this time requiring a costly environmental impact study before approving his expansion.

He stormed into the office where Selene was organizing paperwork. "Look at dis nonsense!" he exclaimed, slamming the letter onto the desk.

She picked it up, her eyes scanning the contents. "Another hurdle?" she sighed.

"Dem really trying fi push mi outta business! How mi supposed to afford dis study? It's not just the cost—it's di time it will take," Marcus fumed.

Selene reached out to touch his arm gently. "Marcus, I know it's frustrating, but we need to stay calm and figure out our next move."

He paced the small room, hands clenched into fists. "Every time mi try move forward, dem put up roadblocks! Mi feel like giving up."

"Don't say dat," she insisted. "Remember what Uncle Roy always seh: 'When trouble tek you, pickney shut fit yuh.' We have to think smart."

He took a deep breath, the tension in his shoulders slowly easing. "Yuh right. Mi can't let dem see mi sweat."

Just then, Uncle Roy entered, his walking stick tapping rhythmically against the floor. "Mi hear yuh got another letter," he said knowingly.

Marcus nodded. "They want an environmental impact study now. Dat's time and money mi nuh have."

Uncle Roy settled into a chair. "Marcus, bureaucracy is a game. Yuh cyaan fight it with anger. We need fi outsmart dem."

"How? Every step forward feels like two steps back," Marcus lamented.

"We'll find a way. Maybe there's assistance available fi small businesses like yours," Selene suggested.

Uncle Roy tapped his chin thoughtfully. "Perhaps. And we need to rally di community more than ever now."

Marcus looked between them, a flicker of hope igniting. "Alright. Let's regroup and plan our next move."

The Rival's Next Move – Hutchinson's Sabotage

A few days later, Marcus was at the garage when Junior, one of his mechanics, approached him with a concerned expression. "Boss, yuh might want to see dis," he said, handing over a copy of a local newspaper.

The headline read: "Local Garage Under Investigation for Environmental Violations."

Marcus's eyes widened as he read the article, which insinuated that his garage was responsible for oil leaks contaminating nearby soil and water sources.

"Dis is madness! None of dis is true!" he exclaimed.

Just then, Jasmine burst into the garage, phone in hand. "Marcus, have you seen the news?"

"Yes, and it's all lies," he gritted his teeth.

"Word on the street is that Hutchinson is behind dis. He's been spreading rumors and now this article," Jasmine informed him.

Marcus slammed his fist onto the workbench. "So yuh telling mi, dis man really a pay people fi mek mi business fail?"

"Looks like it. He's trying to turn public opinion against you," Jasmine said.

Uncle Roy, who had been standing nearby, stepped forward. "Business is war sometimes, Marcus. But di smartest soldier nuh rush di battlefield without a plan."

Marcus took a deep breath, attempting to steady his emotions. "So what do we do?"

"We need to counteract dis negative press and show di truth. Transparency is key," Jasmine advised.

Uncle Roy nodded. "And we must proceed strategically. Di loudest man in di room nuh always di strongest."

"Alright. Let's fight back, but with wisdom," Marcus agreed.

Marcus's Counterattack – Building Influence

Over the next week, Marcus and his team launched a community outreach campaign. They organized a free vehicle maintenance workshop, drawing in locals and demonstrating the garage's commitment to the community.

During the event, satisfied customers shared their testimonies.

"Marcus always takes care of us. His garage is trustworthy," Mrs. Thompson praised.

"He taught mi nephew the basics of auto repair. Keeping youths off the streets," another man added.

Jasmine coordinated with local media, ensuring that positive stories about Marcus's garage were featured in newspapers and on radio shows.

A popular radio host invited Marcus for an interview.

"Tell us about the challenges you've been facing," the host prompted.

Marcus took a deep breath. "We've been dealing with some unfounded accusations, but di truth is, my garage operates with integrity and care for di environment and community."

He continued, "We nuh just fix cars—we build relationships and support our neighbors. Our doors are always open."

The host nodded appreciatively. "It's clear you're passionate about your work and community. We're glad to have you here sharing your side."

After the interview, Marcus felt a renewed sense of purpose.

Back at the garage, Selene hugged him tightly. "You were amazing!"

He smiled. "Hutchinson using money? Fine. We're using di people!"

Uncle Roy chuckled. "You've turned di tide, Marcus. Let dem see di truth—your garage benefits everyone."

The Final Showdown – Facing the Zoning Board

A formal hearing with the zoning board was scheduled, and tensions were high. The room was filled with officials, community members, Marcus's supporters, and, of course, Hutchinson.

Marcus adjusted his tie nervously. Selene squeezed his hand. "You've got this," she whispered.

Jasmine handed him a neatly organized portfolio. "Everything you need is here. Stick to the facts, stay composed."

Uncle Roy gave him a reassuring nod. "Remember, 'Calm water runs deep.'"

The chairman of the zoning board called the meeting to order. "We are here to address the concerns regarding Mr. Marcus Thomas's application for expansion and the recent allegations against his business."

Hutchinson's lawyer was the first to speak, presenting a skewed narrative meant to undermine Marcus.

When it was Marcus's turn, he stood confidently. "Esteemed members of the board, I've operated my garage with utmost integrity for years. The allegations against me are false, aimed at thwarting my progress."

He presented evidence of his compliance with environmental standards, letters of support from the community, and his plans for sustainable expansion.

"Our garage not only adheres to all regulations but also contributes positively to the community by providing jobs and supporting youth programs," he asserted.

Board members whispered among themselves. One cleared her throat. "We've received numerous messages of support on your behalf, Mr. Thomas. Your commitment to environmental stewardship and community service is commendable."

Another member, however, seemed skeptical. "But what of the environmental impact study?"

Marcus responded, "I have initiated the process for the study and am committed to addressing any concerns that arise. However, I believe the additional requirements were introduced unfairly."

The chairman nodded. "Thank you, Mr. Thomas. We will deliberate and inform you of our decision soon."

As the meeting adjourned, Hutchinson approached Marcus with a thin smile. "Impressive performance, but don't get your hopes up."

Marcus met his gaze steadily. "Di truth always comes out in the end."

Hutchinson shrugged. "We'll see about that."

Cliffhanger

The following day, Marcus received a call from one of his suppliers.

"Marcus, I'm sorry, but we have to cancel our contract," the supplier said regretfully.

"What? Why?" Marcus asked, shocked.

"Pressure from above, if you catch my drift. We can't risk losing other clients," the supplier admitted before hanging up.

Marcus felt the weight of the new setback. Hutchinson was trying to choke his business by cutting off supplies.

He gathered his team. "We have another problem. Hutchinson is threatening our suppliers."

Selene shook her head in disbelief. "He's relentless!"

Jasmine crossed her arms. "We'll find alternative suppliers. He can't shut us down that easily."

Uncle Roy placed a reassuring hand on Marcus's shoulder. "Remember, 'When one door closes, another opens.' We must stay resilient."

Marcus gazed at his friends and allies, determination hardening his features. "Then that's exactly what we'll do. We fight on."

Key Financial Lessons Woven into the Story

1. **Leverage Influence in Business**
   a. Marcus learns that success isn't just about financial capital but also about building strong relationships and a positive reputation within the community.
2. **Strategic Thinking Wins Over Emotion**
   a. Instead of reacting impulsively to Hutchinson's provocations, Marcus adopts a strategic approach to counteract his rival's moves.
3. **Community is Wealth**
   a. By garnering the support of his customers and neighbors, Marcus strengthens his position and demonstrates the power of collective backing.
4. **Persistence is Key**
   a. Marcus faces continuous challenges but remains steadfast, understanding that perseverance is essential for long-term success.
5. **Business is a Long Game**

a. He recognizes that quick fixes are not sustainable and that thoughtful, long-term strategies will secure his business's future.

Thoughts

Marcus's journey highlights the realities of entrepreneurship—the obstacles, the competition, and the necessity of resilience. Through community support and strategic action, he stands firm against those who seek to undermine him.

As Marcus contends with supply chain sabotage and awaits the zoning board's decision, the stakes have never been higher. Will his perseverance pay off? Can he outsmart Hutchinson's relentless schemes?

Discover the outcome in the next chapter as Marcus's fight for his business reaches a critical climax, revealing the true power of unity and strategic thinking.

Chapter 6: The Breaking Point— Marcus's Biggest Test Yet

The Zoning Board's Final Decision

The sun hung low in the Kingston sky, casting long shadows over the city. Marcus stood outside the municipal building, his heart pounding like a drum. Selene was beside him, her hand gently squeezing his for support. Jasmine and Uncle Roy were there too, offering steadfast solidarity.

"Dem called us in fi di final decision," Marcus said, his voice tinged with apprehension.

"Whatever happens in there, remember we're with yuh," Selene assured him.

He took a deep breath. "Let's do dis."

Inside the grand chamber, the atmosphere was formal and tense. The zoning board members sat behind a long mahogany table, their expressions unreadable. Hutchinson was there as well, seated smugly in the back, a faint smirk playing on his lips.

The chairman cleared his throat. "Mr. Thomas, thank you for attending this hearing. We've reviewed your application, the environmental impact study, and all supplementary materials you've provided."

Marcus nodded respectfully. "Thank you for your time, Chairman."

Another board member, a stern-looking woman with sharp glasses, interjected. "However, there have been concerns raised about your compliance with certain regulations."

Marcus felt a knot tighten in his stomach. "I've endeavored to meet all requirements to di best of mi ability."

The chairman glanced at his notes. "Indeed, your efforts are noted. But a recent report suggests potential issues with your building's structural integrity and safety protocols."

Marcus exchanged a confused glance with Selene. "Sir, mi not aware of any such issues. Our building passed all inspections."

A board member to the left leaned forward. "These concerns were brought to our attention by an anonymous source."

From the corner of his eye, Marcus saw Hutchinson suppress a grin.

Jasmine stood up. "With all due respect, Chairman, it seems these allegations are unfounded and possibly malicious in nature."

The chairman sighed. "Be that as it may, we cannot proceed without addressing them."

Uncle Roy whispered to Marcus, "Stay calm, son. Dis is a play to unsettle yuh."

Marcus took a deep breath. "Chairman, is there any way to verify these claims promptly? Delaying di decision further will severely impact mi business."

Just then, one of the board members—a dignified elderly man—spoke up. "If I may, I've personally reviewed Mr. Thomas's compliance documents. Everything appears to be in order. Perhaps we should consider the possibility of undue interference."

A murmur spread through the room.

The chairman nodded slowly. "You raise a valid point. Given the community support for Mr. Thomas and the lack of concrete evidence against him, I propose we move to a vote."

Marcus held his breath as the board members cast their votes. The tension was palpable.

"By a majority decision, the board approves Mr. Thomas's application for expansion," the chairman declared.

Relief and joy washed over Marcus. "Thank you, Chairman. Yuh won't regret dis."

Hutchinson's face darkened, his smug demeanor evaporating.

As they exited the building, cheers erupted from friends and community members waiting outside.

Selene threw her arms around Marcus. "You did it!"

He hugged her tightly. "We did it."

Uncle Roy patted his back. "Di battle won, but di war nuh over."

Marcus nodded. "Mi know. Hutchinson won't back down so easily."

The Rival's Last Stand—Hutchinson's Ultimate Sabotage

Victory was sweet but short-lived. Within days, Marcus began receiving cancellation calls from long-time customers.

"Sorry, Marcus, mi can't bring mi car in tomorrow," one customer said hesitantly.

"Everything alright?" Marcus inquired.

"Yeah, but mi hear tings... don't want any trouble," the customer mumbled before hanging up.

Confused and concerned, Marcus gathered his team.

"Something's off. Customers cancelling, suppliers delaying orders without explanation," he said.

Junior chimed in, "Boss, mi hear rumors that we're under investigation again."

Marcus's jaw clenched. "Hutchinson is behind dis. He's spreading lies to ruin us."

Jasmine stormed into the office, her expression grave. "Just got word that our biggest contract is under review. They're considering pulling out."

Selene shook her head. "This is getting out of hand!"

Marcus slammed his fist on the table. "If mi lose dis business, mi lose everything."

Uncle Roy stepped forward. "Then we don't lose, Marcus. We fight smart. And we win."

"How? He's attacking from all sides," Marcus said, frustration seeping into his voice.

"By staying one step ahead. Let's reach out to our customers directly, reassure dem. Transparency is key," Jasmine suggested.

"And we need fi find alternative suppliers, even if it costs more for now," Selene added.

Marcus nodded. "Alright. Time fi damage control."

They launched a campaign, personally contacting customers to address any concerns.

"Don't believe di false rumors. We're fully compliant and here to serve yuh," Marcus assured them.

Many customers appreciated the outreach, but the seed of doubt had been planted in others.

Meanwhile, Hutchinson escalated his efforts, threatening legal action to halt Marcus's expansion, citing fabricated safety concerns.

Marcus met with Mr. Edwards, his lawyer. "Can he do dis?"

"He's leveraging technicalities to stall you. It's a common tactic to drain resources and morale," Mr. Edwards explained.

"Mi funds are already stretched thin," Marcus admitted.

Uncle Roy placed a hand on his shoulder. "Remember, 'When di going gets tough, di tough get going.' We need a new strategy."

The Power Move—Marcus Outmaneuvers Hutchinson

Late one evening, as Marcus sat contemplating his next move, his phone rang.

"Marcus Thomas speaking."

"Good evening, Mr. Thomas. This is Mr. Sinclair from First Caribbean Bank. I believe we can assist each other."

Marcus sat up straight. "I'm listening."

"I've been following your situation. Our institution values community-oriented businesses like yours. We'd like to offer financial backing to help you through this challenging period," Mr. Sinclair proposed.

"What's the catch?" Marcus asked cautiously.

"No catch. In exchange, we ask that you consider partnering with us for future community development projects," Mr. Sinclair explained.

Marcus felt a glimmer of hope. "That sounds promising."

The next day, he met with Mr. Sinclair. The partnership would provide the capital needed to secure new suppliers and sustain operations despite Hutchinson's sabotage.

Furthermore, Mr. Sinclair had influence in circles Hutchinson did not.

"I also have contacts in the regulatory bodies. Perhaps it's time to shed light on any unethical practices affecting your business," Mr. Sinclair suggested.

With this newfound alliance, Marcus felt the tides turning.

He and his team ramped up their efforts. They secured new suppliers, even negotiating better terms in the long run.

Jasmine coordinated a media piece exposing the underhanded tactics used against Marcus, without directly naming Hutchinson but making the implications clear.

Public sympathy swung heavily in Marcus's favor.

One afternoon, as Marcus was reviewing paperwork, a knock sounded at his office door.

"Come in," he called.

To his surprise, Hutchinson entered, his demeanor noticeably less arrogant.

"What do you want?" Marcus asked coldly.

Hutchinson sighed. "Seems you've made some powerful friends."

Marcus leaned back in his chair. "Hard work and integrity attract good company."

Hutchinson shifted uncomfortably. "Perhaps we've gotten off on the wrong foot. Maybe we can find a way to... coexist."

Marcus eyed him carefully. "You mean after you tried to destroy mi business?"

"Just business, nothing personal," Hutchinson shrugged.

"Well, mi take it very personal when mi community and livelihood are attacked," Marcus retorted.

Hutchinson frowned. "You're not making this easy."

"Success nuh come easy. Maybe it's time you consider your own actions," Marcus suggested.

Hutchinson's eyes flashed with annoyance. "This isn't over."

"Maybe not for you, but for me, mi moving forward," Marcus replied firmly.

As Hutchinson left, Uncle Roy stepped into the office, having overheard the exchange.

"Di loudest man in di room nuh always di strongest. But di smartest one always win," Uncle Roy remarked.

Marcus nodded. "Let Hutchinson play checkers. We're playing chess."

The Final Battle—Marcus's Last Gamble

Despite the strategic victories, the financial strain was mounting. The increased costs of new suppliers and legal fees were taking their toll.

Marcus gathered his team. "Mi have an idea, but it's risky."

Selene looked at him intently. "Tell us."

"I want to invest in a state-of-the-art diagnostic system. It will set us apart from any other garage in Kingston," he explained.

Jasmine considered this. "It would attract more customers, especially those with high-end vehicles."

"But it's a significant investment," Selene cautioned. "If it doesn't yield returns quickly, we could be in trouble."

Marcus met their gazes steadily. "Dis is it. If mi fail, mi done. If mi win, mi change everything."

Uncle Roy smiled knowingly. "Fortune favors di bold."

They decided to proceed. Marcus secured additional funding through Mr. Sinclair's connections, putting everything on the line.

The new system was installed, and a grand reopening was planned. Invitations were sent out to the community, local businesses, and media.

The night before the event, disaster struck.

Marcus received a frantic call from Junior. "Boss, there's a fire at di garage!"

His heart sank. "What? I'm on mi way!"

He raced to the scene to find firefighters battling flames engulfing a portion of the garage. The air was thick with smoke, the acrid smell stinging his lungs.

Selene arrived shortly after, tears in her eyes. "How did this happen?"

"Mi nuh know," Marcus replied, despair creeping in.

A firefighter approached. "We got it under control, but there's significant damage."

Marcus ran a hand over his face. "Thank you for your help."

As the night wore on, it became clear that someone had sabotaged the garage.

"This can't be a coincidence," Jasmine said grimly. "Hutchinson must be behind this."

"We have no proof," Marcus said wearily.

Just then, a young man approached hesitantly. "Mr. Thomas?"

"Yes?" Marcus replied.

"I... I saw someone around di garage earlier. He was acting suspicious," the young man admitted.

"Can you describe him?" Jasmine asked quickly.

He nodded. "I think it was Mr. Hutchinson's assistant. I've seen him before."

Marcus's eyes hardened. "Thank you. This means a lot."

Cliffhanger

With evidence of foul play, Marcus faced a critical decision.

"Do we press charges and get embroiled in a lengthy legal battle, or focus on rebuilding?" Selene asked.

Marcus looked around at the remnants of his dream, then at the faces of those who stood by him.

"Dis is it. Mi can't let fear or anger dictate mi actions," he stated firmly.

Uncle Roy stepped forward. "So what's the plan, son?"

Marcus squared his shoulders. "We rebuild, better than before. And we let di law handle Hutchinson."

Jasmine placed a hand on his arm. "Are you sure? This could be the final blow."

He nodded resolutely. "Failure nuh inna wi blood. We press forward!"

As dawn broke, casting rays of hope over the battered garage, Marcus and his team prepared to face the biggest challenge yet.

Key Financial Lessons Woven into the Story

1. **Strategic Negotiation**
   a. Marcus learns to negotiate under pressure, securing investments and alliances that protect his business.
2. **Crisis Management**
   a. He handles sabotage and uncertainty with composure, focusing on solutions rather than dwelling on problems.
3. **The Power of Long-Term Thinking**
   a. By prioritizing sustainable growth over short-term gains, Marcus positions his business for enduring success.
4. **Networking and Business Alliances**
   a. Leveraging relationships becomes crucial, illustrating that connections are as valuable as capital.
5. **Calculated Risk-Taking**

a. Marcus understands that significant achievements require bold decisions, balancing risk with strategic planning.

Thoughts

Marcus stands at a crossroads, facing the aftermath of the sabotage with unwavering determination. The culmination of his trials tests not only his business acumen but his spirit. His journey underscores that in the realm of entrepreneurship, resilience, integrity, and strategic alliances are the pillars of lasting success.

Will Marcus's unwavering resolve and strategic planning be enough to overcome this final challenge? Can he rebuild his dream amidst the ashes and secure a future free from his rival's shadow?

Join us in the next chapter as Marcus fights to rise from the ruins, embodying the true spirit of perseverance and inspiring a community to stand with him.

Chapter 7: Rising from the Ashes—Rebuilding After Devastation

Picking Up the Pieces—The Aftermath of the Fire

The morning sun cast a bleak light over what remained of Marcus's garage. The smell of smoke still lingered in the air, mingling with the scent of damp ash. Charred beams jutted upward like the skeletal fingers of a giant, grasping at the sky. Marcus stood silently amidst the ruins, his heart heavy with a mix of sorrow and determination.

His employees gathered around him, their faces etched with worry. Junior shuffled his feet, hesitating before speaking. "Boss, wha wi a go do now? Wi nuh have no place fi work."

Marcus took a deep breath, his gaze sweeping over the wreckage. "Mi nah lie, tings rough right now. But wi cyaan give up. Wi haffi find a way fi move forward."

Selene approached, her eyes reflecting his pain. "Marcus, di insurance money won't cover everything. Wi haffi consider all options."

He nodded, the weight of the situation pressing down on him. "Mi know. Wi might have to scale down fi a while."

Jasmine joined them, her expression thoughtful. "What if wi involve di community? Set up a crowdfunding campaign fi help rebuild?"

Uncle Roy stepped forward, his walking stick tapping lightly on the debris-strewn ground. "Marcus, a true businessman nuh fold when tings get rough. Wi adapt, wi survive."

Marcus sighed deeply. "Uncle Roy, mi tired of fighting. Every step mi tek, it feel like di world push mi back."

Uncle Roy placed a firm hand on his shoulder. "Den push back harder. Yuh not just building a garage. Yuh building a legacy."

The words resonated within him. He straightened his shoulders, a flicker of resolve igniting. "Alright. Wi start by reaching out to di community."

Selene smiled softly. "Dat's di spirit."

The Rebuilding Strategy—Thinking Beyond the Garage

In the days that followed, Marcus gathered his closest allies around his dining table, now transformed into a makeshift planning hub. Blueprints, notes, and financial statements were spread out before them.

"Rebuilding di garage as it was nuh enough," Marcus stated. "Wi need fi think bigger."

Jasmine leaned in, intrigued. "What yuh have in mind?"

"Suppose wi transform di garage into a service and training center? Help di youths learn a trade while providing top-notch service," Marcus proposed.

Selene's eyes lit up. "Dat could attract attention from investors interested in social entrepreneurship."

Uncle Roy nodded approvingly. "Now yuh thinking like a visionary."

Mr. Edwards adjusted his glasses. "Legally, wi can file a formal complaint against Hutchinson fi di sabotage. It might take time, but justice will prevail."

Marcus considered this. "Mi focus right now is rebuilding. If wi can secure funding, wi can turn dis tragedy into opportunity."

Jasmine tapped her pen thoughtfully. "There's a grant available for community development projects. Wi can apply."

Selene added, "Wi could also consider a business loan. I know it's a risk, but it could pay off."

Marcus hesitated. "Taking on debt after everything dat happen... it's risky."

Uncle Roy gave him a steady look. "Sometimes yuh haffi step out pon faith. Is di difference between surviving and thriving."

Marcus exhaled slowly. "Alright. Wi explore all options."

The Community's Power—Turning Setback into Strength

Word of Marcus's plight spread throughout the community. One morning, as he arrived at the remains of the garage, he was met with a surprising sight. A crowd had gathered—customers, former apprentices, even fellow business owners.

Mrs. Thompson approached him with a warm smile. "Marcus, wi hear what happen. Wi here fi help."

A young man stepped forward. "Yuh teach mi fi fix mi first car. Least mi can do is lend a hand."

Junior grinned. "Boss, wi ready fi work. Just tell wi what fi do."

Emotion welled up in Marcus's chest. "Mi caah express how grateful mi am. Together, wi can make dis happen."

Jasmine seized the moment, capturing footage and interviews to share with the media. Her efforts brought wider attention to Marcus's story, highlighting both the injustice he faced and the resilience of the community.

A few days later, Marcus received a call from Mr. Sinclair. "Marcus, your story has reached some influential ears. Mr. Bennett, a prominent business mogul, is interested in meeting with you."

Marcus was astonished. "What would someone like him want wid mi?"

"He's impressed by your determination and community impact. This could be a significant opportunity," Mr. Sinclair explained.

As Marcus pondered this development, doubt flickered in his mind. He confided in Selene that evening.

"Mi nuh know if mi ready fi all dis. What if mi fail again?" he admitted.

She took his hand gently. "Marcus, yuh community believe in yuh. Now di question is—do yuh believe in yuhself?"

He looked into her eyes, finding strength there. "Hutchinson still out deh, waiting fi mi fail."

"Den give him something unexpected—success," she encouraged.

The Grand Reopening—A New Era Begins

Months of tireless effort culminated in the grand reopening of Marcus's garage. The building stood proudly, a modern facility with expanded service bays and a dedicated training center for aspiring mechanics.

Banners hung from the entrance, and a festive atmosphere filled the air as people gathered to celebrate.

Marcus stood before the crowd, emotion tightening his throat. "Thank yuh all fi standing by mi. Dis garage nuh just belong to mi—it belong to all a wi."

Cheers erupted as he cut the ceremonial ribbon. As guests toured the new facility, they marveled at the state-of-the-art equipment and the enthusiastic trainees eager to learn.

Mr. Bennett approached Marcus, shaking his hand firmly. "Impressive work, Mr. Thomas. You've built something truly special here."

"Thank yuh, sir. It wouldn't be possible without di support of everyone here," Marcus replied humbly.

Mr. Bennett smiled. "I'd like to discuss the possibility of partnering on future projects. Your vision aligns with initiatives I'm passionate about."

Jasmine beamed. "Marcus, dis could open so many doors!"

Uncle Roy nodded sagely. "Yuh turn di worst time into di best opportunity."

Selene hugged Marcus tightly. "I'm so proud of yuh."

Just then, Hutchinson appeared at the edge of the crowd, his expression unreadable. He approached Marcus slowly.

"Congratulations," Hutchinson said flatly.

Marcus met his gaze steadily. "Thank you."

Hutchinson hesitated before admitting, "I underestimated you."

"Seems so," Marcus replied calmly.

A flicker of something—regret, perhaps—passed over Hutchinson's face. "Maybe competition drove mi to make poor choices."

"Every man responsible fi him own actions," Marcus stated.

Hutchinson gave a curt nod before walking away, disappearing into the sea of faces.

Uncle Roy clapped a hand on Marcus's shoulder. "Dis just di beginning."

Marcus smiled wistfully. "Indeed it is."

Cliffhanger—Marcus's Next Challenge

As the celebrations wound down, Mr. Bennett pulled Marcus aside.

"There's an opportunity I'd like you to consider," he began. "I'm expanding operations and need someone with your talents to oversee a series of auto service centers across di island."

Marcus's eyes widened. "Dat's a huge undertaking."

Mr. Bennett nodded. "It comes with significant investment and, of course, risk. But I believe you're the man for the job."

That evening, Marcus sat with Selene, the weight of the offer heavy on his mind.

"Every dream comes wid risk. Now di question is—how big mi willing fi dream?" he mused.

Selene took his hand. "Whatever you decide, I'll be right here by your side."

He gazed out at the stars twinkling above, the vastness of possibilities stretching before him.

Key Financial Lessons Woven into the Story

1. **Resilience is the Heart of Entrepreneurship**
    a. Marcus learns that perseverance in the face of adversity is essential for success.
2. **Diversification is Key to Long-Term Growth**
    a. By expanding his garage into a training center, he creates additional revenue streams and community value.
3. **Leveraging Community Support and Social Capital**
    a. The power of relationships and goodwill proves invaluable in rebuilding and advancing his business.
4. **Strategic Risk-Taking**
    a. Marcus considers bold moves that could significantly impact his future, weighing potential risks and rewards.

Thoughts

Marcus's journey from devastation to triumph showcases the transformative power of resilience, community, and visionary leadership. His story inspires us to see obstacles as opportunities and to believe in the possibilities that lie beyond our fears.

As Marcus stands on the brink of a new horizon, he faces a monumental decision that could redefine his future. Will he seize the chance to expand his legacy across the island, or will he choose to nurture what he's built at home?

Discover the path he takes in the next chapter, where dreams soar, and new challenges await.

Chapter 8: The Next Level— Building a Business Empire

The Decision—Growth vs. Stability

The golden glow of the setting sun bathed Marcus's garage, casting long shadows that mirrored his contemplative mood. He stood on the balcony of his home, overlooking the bustling streets of Kingston. The rhythmic sounds of life—laughter, distant music, the hum of traffic— usually brought him comfort. Tonight, they were drowned out by the whirlwind of thoughts in his mind.

Selene joined him, her presence a calming balm. "Yuh been quiet since wi left Mr. Bennett's office," she observed gently.

Marcus sighed, rubbing the back of his neck. "It's a big decision, Selene. Expanding across di island... it's massive."

She nodded. "Mi know. It could change everything."

"Exactly. But at what cost?" he mused.

She looked at him earnestly. "What does your heart tell yuh?"

"Mi torn," he admitted. "On one hand, dis is a chance to elevate everything wi worked for. On di other, mi worry 'bout losing control, losing what makes di garage special."

Before she could respond, Uncle Roy's familiar voice called from below. "Marcus! Come down yah, man. Mi bring some of dat sorrel yuh love."

They made their way downstairs to find Uncle Roy and Jasmine seated at the kitchen table, animatedly discussing plans.

"Uncle Roy, Jasmine, good to see y'all," Marcus greeted them.

Jasmine leaned forward, excitement gleaming in her eyes. "Marcus, dis opportunity with Mr. Bennett is huge! Yuh have to consider it seriously."

He nodded slowly. "Trust mi, it's all mi been thinking about."

Uncle Roy sipped his sorrel thoughtfully. "Marcus, mi proud a yuh. But expansion nuh mean success. Sometimes more money bring more problems."

"What yuh mean?" Marcus asked, searching his mentor's face.

"Remember di stories of those who grow too fast, only to collapse because dem couldn't manage di scale," Uncle Roy cautioned. "Yuh have a good ting here. Don't lose sight of it."

Selene placed a supportive hand on Marcus's shoulder. "He's right. We need to weigh di risks carefully."

Jasmine interjected, "But opportunities like dis don't come twice, Marcus. If yuh nuh grab it, somebody else will."

A heavy silence settled over the room as Marcus grappled with their words.

"Mi need time fi think," he finally said.

The Challenges of Scaling a Business

The next morning, Marcus met with Mr. Bennett at a sleek office overlooking the city. The environment was polished and sophisticated— a stark contrast to the grease and grit of the garage.

"Marcus, glad you could make it," Mr. Bennett greeted warmly, extending a hand.

"Thank you for inviting me," Marcus replied, taking a seat.

Mr. Bennett began outlining the proposal. "We plan to open service centers in every major town across di island. With your expertise and reputation, we want you to lead this initiative."

"It sounds ambitious," Marcus remarked.

"It is. But with ambition comes great rewards," Mr. Bennett smiled. "Of course, it would require you to delegate more, hire managers, and trust others to uphold your standards."

Marcus shifted uncomfortably. "Mi always been hands-on. Letting go won't be easy."

"I understand. But think of di impact you could have. Elevating di auto repair industry nationwide," Mr. Bennett encouraged.

"What's di catch?" Marcus asked bluntly.

Mr. Bennett's smile faltered slightly. "Well, there is another party interested in this venture—a foreign investor looking to establish a chain of auto shops here."

Marcus's eyes narrowed. "If I decline, they'll take my place?"

"Possibly. And to be frank, they might not have di community's best interests at heart," Mr. Bennett admitted. "We're offering you this opportunity because we believe in supporting local talent."

Marcus leaned back, processing the information. "Dis is a lot to consider."

"Take your time, but not too long," Mr. Bennett advised.

The Ethical Dilemma—Business vs. Community

Back at the garage, Marcus gathered his team. Selene, Uncle Roy, Jasmine, and his loyal employees sat in a circle, the atmosphere thick with anticipation.

"Mi need fi talk to y'all about something important," Marcus began. "Mr. Bennett offered me a deal to expand across di island."

Cheers erupted from some, while others exchanged uncertain glances.

"Dat's amazing news!" Junior exclaimed.

"But there's more to it," Marcus continued. "Expanding like dis means I can't be involved in every detail. We'd have to trust new people to run things di right way."

Selene spoke up, concern evident in her eyes. "Marcus, are yuh sure dat dis expansion won't compromise di values we've built here?"

Uncle Roy added, "Di best business nuh just mek money, it build futures. Will dis move allow yuh to keep uplifting di community?"

Marcus scratched his head. "That's what mi wrestling with. If we don't take dis chance, a foreign investor might come in and push out small garages like ours."

Jasmine leaned forward. "Exactly. If yuh nuh tek control, somebody else will. An' dem might not have di community at heart."

Silence settled as everyone pondered the gravity of the situation.

"Mi worry 'bout quality control," Marcus admitted. "Expanding too fast could lead to mistakes. And what happens to our staff if tings go wrong?"

Selene reached for his hand. "Mi love yuh ambition, Marcus. But yuh sure dis nuh come at a cost?"

He looked into her eyes, conflicted. "Mi want to do right by everyone."

Uncle Roy gave a reassuring smile. "Sometimes di hardest choices lead to di greatest outcomes. But yuh haffi trust yuh gut."

The Business War—A New Threat Arises

News broke that a foreign investor planned to launch a series of high-end auto repair shops across Jamaica, threatening to overshadow local businesses.

Marcus watched the announcement on television with a sinking feeling. The investor, a slick businessman named Mr. Thompson, spoke confidently about "modernizing" the industry.

"This is exactly what we feared," Jasmine said, frustration lacing her voice.

Junior burst into the office. "Boss, people talking 'bout how these new shops will put us outta business!"

Marcus stood, determination hardening his gaze. "Not if we have anything to say about it."

Selene looked at him questioningly. "What's your plan?"

"Wi need to unite di local garages. Strength in numbers," Marcus declared.

Uncle Roy nodded approvingly. "Now yuh thinking like a true leader."

They spent the next few days reaching out to other small garage owners. At a gathering in a community center, Marcus addressed the group.

"Dem a bring big money, but wi have something dem nuh have—loyalty an' trust," he emphasized. "If we band together, share resources, and support one another, we can compete."

One owner, Mr. Williams, raised a concern. "But how we fi match their prices and fancy equipment?"

"We may not have di same funds, but we offer personalized service and real relationships with our customers," Marcus countered. "Plus, we can explore new ideas—like mobile repair services, loyalty programs, and community events."

Murmurs of agreement spread through the room.

Jasmine added, "And by creating a network, we can negotiate better deals with suppliers."

Encouraged, the group began to see the potential in unity.

Marcus Makes His Decision

With renewed purpose, Marcus met with Mr. Bennett one last time.

"Mr. Bennett, I appreciate your offer, but I can't accept it as it stands," Marcus stated firmly.

Mr. Bennett raised an eyebrow. "Oh? And why is that?"

"Mi want to expand, but not at di cost of mi values. I'd like to propose a partnership—on mi terms," Marcus explained.

Intrigued, Mr. Bennett leaned forward. "I'm listening."

Marcus outlined his vision: investing in local garages to create a network that maintained high standards while preserving community ties. He emphasized sustainable growth, ethical practices, and mutual support.

"This approach could not only compete with di foreign investor but also uplift communities across Jamaica," Marcus concluded.

Mr. Bennett considered the proposal thoughtfully. "You're a bold man, Marcus. I admire that. Alright, let's explore this partnership further."

Relief and excitement washed over Marcus. "Thank you for giving this a chance."

As the sun set, Marcus stood atop a hill overlooking the city, Selene by his side.

"You did it," she whispered, pride evident in her voice.

He smiled softly. "Dis just di beginning. There's so much more to build."

In the distance, Hutchinson watched them, a hint of a smile tugging at his lips. He approached slowly.

"Marcus," Hutchinson called out.

Marcus turned, surprised. "Hutchinson."

"I heard about your plans. Can't say I'm not impressed," Hutchinson admitted.

"Thank you," Marcus replied cautiously.

"Perhaps there's room for an old rival in your network?" Hutchinson offered, extending a hand.

Marcus considered him for a moment before shaking his hand firmly. "There's always room for those willing to work together."

A newfound respect passed between them.

Cliffhanger—Marcus's Next Challenge

The next morning, a crisp envelope arrived at Marcus's office, bearing an international postmark. Curiosity piqued, he opened it to find a letter from a prestigious automotive corporation based overseas.

"Dear Mr. Thomas,

We have been following your innovative work in Jamaica and believe your model could revolutionize the auto repair industry globally. We invite you to discuss an opportunity to take your vision worldwide.

Sincerely,

Global Auto Corp."

Marcus's heart raced as he shared the news with Selene.

"Jamaica mi heart, but maybe mi destiny bigger dan mi ever imagine," he murmured.

She took his hand, her eyes reflecting both excitement and caution. "Are you ready for dis next step?"

He gazed out the window, the horizon stretching endlessly. "I guess we'll find out."

Key Financial & Business Lessons in Chapter 8

1. **Smart Scaling and Strategic Growth**
    a. Marcus learns that expansion requires careful planning to maintain quality and uphold core values.
2. **The Power of Ethical Leadership**

a. He realizes that true success comes from staying true to his principles, even when faced with lucrative opportunities.
3. **Competitive Strategy Against Big Corporations**
    a. By uniting local businesses, Marcus creates a formidable alliance that leverages community strengths against larger competitors.
4. **Networking and Business Alliances**
    a. Collaboration over competition becomes a key strategy, highlighting the importance of partnerships.
5. **Knowing When to Say No to Bad Deals**
    a. Marcus understands that not every opportunity aligns with his vision, and sometimes declining is the wiser choice.

Thoughts

Marcus stands at the precipice of unprecedented growth, his journey reflecting the complexities of ambition balanced with integrity. As he contemplates taking his vision to a global stage, he must once again navigate uncharted waters, confronting new challenges that test the very core of his beliefs.

Will Marcus embrace the international opportunity and expand his impact beyond Jamaica's shores? Can he maintain his commitment to community and ethical practices on a global scale?

Join us in the next chapter as Marcus faces the exciting yet daunting prospect of taking his legacy worldwide, and discover the new horizons that await.

Chapter 9: The Global Gamble—Marcus Steps Onto the World Stage

The International Offer—Golden Opportunity or Dangerous Trap?

The gentle hum of the air conditioner was the only sound in the sleek boardroom overlooking the shimmering skyline of Kingston. Marcus sat at the long glass table, a folder containing the offer from Global Auto Corp. resting heavily in his hands. The representatives across from him wore polished smiles, their tailored suits a stark contrast to Marcus's modest attire.

"Mr. Thomas, we are thoroughly impressed with your innovative business model and community impact," Mr. Stevens, the lead executive, began. "We believe that with our resources and your vision, we can replicate this success internationally."

Marcus glanced at the proposal. The numbers were staggering—a lucrative deal that promised exponential growth. But something gnawed at him.

"Dis offer is generous," Marcus acknowledged, his voice steady. "But mi concerned about how much control mi would retain over di business practices and values."

Ms. Chen, another executive, leaned forward. "Naturally, there would be some adjustments to align with our corporate model. Standardization is key at a global scale."

"Adjustments like what?" Marcus inquired.

"Streamlining operations, optimizing costs, perhaps revising your training programs to fit a more universal framework," she explained.

Marcus's brow furrowed. "Mi training programs are tailored fi uplift mi community, provide opportunities fi di youths."

Mr. Stevens smiled diplomatically. "We understand, but certain modifications are necessary for efficiency."

An uneasy feeling settled in Marcus's stomach. "Mi haffi think 'bout dis carefully."

"Of course," Mr. Stevens said, his smile unwavering. "But do consider the magnitude of this opportunity. We look forward to your decision."

Back at home, Marcus sat on the porch, the ocean breeze rustling through the palm trees. Selene joined him, concern etched across her face.

"How did it go?" she asked softly.

He sighed, staring out at the horizon. "Dem offer is tempting, but mi nuh sure mi comfortable wid di terms. Dem want to change di very things dat mek mi business special."

She nodded. "Once yuh sign, can yuh still call dis business yuh own?"

"Exactly. Mi feel like mi could lose mi soul in di process," Marcus admitted.

Uncle Roy shuffled onto the porch, his cane tapping lightly. "Marcus, success nuh just 'bout big money. It's 'bout keeping yuh soul."

"Mi know, Uncle Roy. But di pressure mounting. If mi nuh accept, someone else might step in," Marcus said, his voice heavy.

Just then, Jasmine burst through the door. "Marcus! Dis could put Jamaica on di map! Think of di impact!"

He looked at her, torn. "But at what cost, Jasmine? Mi nuh want fi lose control over mi vision."

She placed a hand on his shoulder. "Maybe there's a way fi negotiate better terms?"

Marcus shook his head. "Dem seem set in their ways. Mi need fi find another path."

The Reality of Global Business—Bigger Risks, Bigger Rewards

Determined to make an informed decision, Marcus attended a seminar on international business at a prestigious hotel in Kingston. The room buzzed with entrepreneurs and industry leaders from around the world.

During a break, he struck up a conversation with Mr. Alvarez, a seasoned businessman from Mexico.

"Expanding globally is no small feat," Mr. Alvarez cautioned. "Cultural differences, supply chain complexities, corporate bureaucracy—it can be overwhelming."

"How do yuh maintain quality across multiple locations?" Marcus asked.

"You must establish strong core values and ensure they are upheld at every level. But even then, it's a challenge," Mr. Alvarez admitted.

Another entrepreneur, Ms. Okoro from Nigeria, joined the conversation. "Be wary of losing your identity. I expanded too quickly once and almost lost the essence of my brand."

Marcus absorbed their words, realizing the enormity of what he was contemplating.

As the seminar concluded, news broke that an international auto conglomerate planned to enter the Jamaican market. The announcement blared from a television in the lobby.

"Global Motors Co. aims to revolutionize Jamaica's auto industry," the reporter declared.

Marcus felt a knot tighten in his chest. "If mi nuh move fast, dem could crush everything mi built."

Returning to the garage, he gathered his team.

"Wi have a new challenge," he announced. "A foreign company plans to dominate di auto repair industry here."

Jasmine's eyes widened. "Dis is serious."

Selene looked at him thoughtfully. "What are you going to do?"

Marcus clenched his fists. "Mi won't let dem take over without a fight."

Jasmine suddenly smiled. "Marcus, what if instead of selling out, yuh create yuh own global brand?"

He looked at her, a spark igniting. "Go on."

"We can leverage di network you've built, expand on your own terms," she elaborated.

Uncle Roy grinned. "Now dat's thinking big."

The Dilemma—Independence vs. Power

That night, Marcus wrestled with his thoughts. The weight of the decision pressed heavily on his shoulders.

He sat at the kitchen table, financial projections and proposals strewn before him. Selene poured two cups of tea, sitting across from him.

"Talk to me," she encouraged.

"Mi torn between partnering wid Global Auto Corp and maintaining mi independence," Marcus confessed. "Partnering could mean instant growth but less control. Going solo is risky."

She reached out, touching his hand. "Remember why you started all this. Di world always looking for di next big thing, but yuh must decide what kind of legacy yuh leaving."

He nodded slowly. "If mi expand di right way, mi can inspire di next generation."

Just then, his phone buzzed. It was Mr. Sinclair.

"Marcus, I have someone you should meet," Mr. Sinclair said cryptically.

The next day, Marcus found himself in the opulent office of Dr. Aisha Campbell, a Jamaican billionaire investor known for her philanthropic ventures and commitment to empowering local businesses.

"Mr. Thomas, your reputation precedes you," she greeted warmly.

"Dr. Campbell, it's an honor," Marcus responded respectfully.

"I've followed your journey. You're a beacon of what Jamaican entrepreneurship can be," she praised. "I understand you're facing a significant decision."

"Yes, ma'am. Mi considering expanding globally but want to keep control and stay true to mi values," he explained.

She smiled. "I believe we can help each other. I can provide the capital and resources for you to expand internationally while ensuring your business remains rooted in Jamaican ownership and principles."

Marcus felt hope surge within him. "You'd do dat?"

"Absolutely. It's time we showcase Jamaican excellence on the world stage, without diluting our identity," Dr. Campbell affirmed.

Marcus's Power Move—Choosing His Own Path

Buoyed by the new possibility, Marcus returned to his team with renewed vigor.

"Mi made mi decision," he announced. "We're going to expand globally on our own terms, with Dr. Campbell's support."

Cheers erupted around the room.

Jasmine grinned. "I knew you'd find a way!"

Selene's eyes shone with pride. "I'm with you all the way."

Uncle Roy gave a satisfied nod. "Yuh making di right choice, son."

They set to work immediately, outlining plans for international expansion while preserving the core values that made their business unique.

They developed training programs for young entrepreneurs in Jamaica, aiming to replicate their success and uplift communities worldwide.

As word spread, the community rallied behind them. Marcus's brand became synonymous with integrity, quality, and empowerment.

Meanwhile, the foreign conglomerate faced stiff resistance from locals loyal to Marcus's vision. Realizing they couldn't outmatch his community support and authentic appeal, they scaled back their plans.

One evening, as the sun dipped below the horizon, Marcus stood atop the newly built headquarters—a sleek testament to his journey.

Hutchinson approached, a genuine smile on his face. "Yuh did it, Marcus. Yuh showed all of us what's possible."

Marcus extended his hand. "Couldn't have done it without the lessons along di way."

They shook hands, the past animosity replaced with mutual respect.

"What's next for you?" Hutchinson asked.

Marcus gazed into the distance. "Dis just di beginning. So much more to achieve."

Cliffhanger—The Final Chapter Awaits

A few weeks later, an elegant invitation arrived at Marcus's office, embossed with gold lettering.

"Dear Mr. Thomas,

You are cordially invited to speak at the Global Entrepreneurship Summit in Geneva. Your insights into sustainable and community-focused business models are highly valued.

Sincerely,

The Summit Committee"

Marcus read the invitation aloud to his team.

Jasmine's eyes widened. "This is huge!"

Selene beamed. "From di small streets of Kingston to di global stage—mi never imagined we'd be here."

Uncle Roy chuckled. "But we always knew you were destined for great things."

Marcus took a deep breath. "But dis is only di beginning."

As he contemplated the journey ahead, a mix of excitement and nervousness coursed through him.

"Time to show di world what Jamaican entrepreneurship is all about," he declared.

Key Financial & Business Lessons in Chapter 9

1. **Building a Global Brand While Keeping Local Identity**
   a. Marcus expands internationally without compromising his core values or relinquishing control.
2. **Understanding the Risks of International Business**
   a. He considers cultural differences, supply chain complexities, and the importance of maintaining consistent quality.
3. **The Power of Independent Growth vs. Selling Out**
   a. By choosing to partner with a like-minded investor, Marcus retains ownership and direction of his company.
4. **Competitive Strategy at a Global Level**
   a. He outmaneuvers a foreign conglomerate by leveraging community support and authentic branding.
5. **Leadership & Vision in Business Expansion**
   a. Marcus mentors young entrepreneurs, fostering a legacy of empowerment and sustainable growth.

Thoughts

Marcus's rise from a humble garage owner to an international business leader embodies the essence of visionary entrepreneurship. His journey underscores the importance of staying true to one's values, the power of community, and the impact of strategic, principled decision-making.

As Marcus prepares to share his story on the world stage, new horizons unfold. Will he inspire global change and forge new alliances that transcend borders?

Join us in the final chapter as Marcus embraces his destiny, shaping not just his future but influencing the world of business itself.

PART 2: GETTING MONEY RIGHT

(Earning, Saving, and Managing Wisely)

Chapter 10: The Art of Earning— Why Every Dollar Counts

Reflecting on the Journey

The morning sun cast a golden hue over Kingston, bathing the city in warmth. Marcus sat on the balcony of his home, sipping a cup of strong Jamaican coffee. The aroma mingled with the salty sea breeze, creating a serene atmosphere. He gazed out at the horizon, the waves crashing rhythmically against the shore.

Selene joined him, her presence as comforting as the rising sun. "Morning, love. Yuh deep in thought," she observed, placing a gentle hand on his shoulder.

He smiled softly. "Just reflecting on how far we've come. From di small garage to now contemplating di global stage."

She nodded, her eyes filled with pride. "It's been an incredible journey. But mi know you—always thinking 'bout what's next."

He chuckled. "Yuh know mi too well. But Selene, amidst all di expansion and big plans, mi realize something."

"What's that?" she asked, curiosity piqued.

"Di importance of earning. Not just making money, but understanding di value of every dollar. How it adds up, how it can work for us or against us," he explained.

She sipped her coffee thoughtfully. "True words. Remember when we struggled to make ends meet? Every dollar mattered then."

"Exactly. And mi think it's time to revisit those lessons. To ensure we and those we mentor understand di art of earning," Marcus declared.

A Heart-to-Heart with Uncle Roy

Later that day, Marcus visited Uncle Roy at his quaint countryside home. The scent of ripe mangoes filled the air as they sat under the shade of a towering ackee tree.

"Marcus, mi boy! What brings yuh dis side of town?" Uncle Roy greeted him warmly.

"Needed some of your wisdom, Uncle Roy. Been thinking 'bout di fundamentals—earning, saving, managing money," Marcus replied.

Uncle Roy stroked his greying beard thoughtfully. "Ah, di basics. Sometimes wi get so caught up in big tings, wi forget di foundation."

"Exactly. Mi want to ensure that as we grow, we don't lose sight of why every dollar counts," Marcus affirmed.

Uncle Roy leaned back in his chair. "Let mi tell yuh a story. When mi was a young man, mi worked di fields from sunrise to sunset. Hard labor, but honest work. Mi used to think if mi just work harder, mi would mek more money."

"Did it work out dat way?" Marcus inquired.

"Not quite. Mi realized dat it's not just 'bout how hard yuh work, but how smart yuh work. Yuh haffi find ways fi mek yuh earnings grow, even while yuh sleep," Uncle Roy explained.

Marcus nodded. "Passive income."

"Precisely. But before yuh reach dat stage, yuh need fi respect every dollar yuh earn. Treat it like a seed dat can grow into a mighty tree if yuh nurture it right," Uncle Roy advised.

Sharing Wisdom with the Team

Back at the headquarters, Marcus gathered his team, including Selene, Jasmine, Junior, and a group of young entrepreneurs he was mentoring.

"Today, I want to talk about di art of earning and why every dollar counts," Marcus began, his voice carrying a blend of passion and sincerity.

Junior raised his hand playfully. "Boss, wi thought earning was just 'bout working and getting paid."

Marcus smiled. "That's part of it, but there's more. Earning isn't just receiving money for work. It's about understanding di value of your time, skills, and how to maximize them."

One of the young entrepreneurs, Keisha, leaned forward. "How do we maximize our earnings when opportunities seem limited?"

"Great question, Keisha. First, identify your skills and talents. What can yuh offer dat others need? Then, look for ways to diversify your income streams," Marcus explained.

Jasmine chimed in, "And don't underestimate di power of negotiation. Know your worth and don't be afraid to ask for it."

Selene added, "Remember, every dollar saved is a dollar earned. Cutting unnecessary expenses boosts your effective earnings."

Marcus nodded in agreement. "And invest in yourself. Education, certifications, learning new trades—all these can increase your earning potential."

Practical Applications

Marcus decided to illustrate his points with real-life examples.

"Let me share a story from mi early days," he began. "When mi started di garage, mi relied solely on fixing cars for income. But then, mi realized I could offer additional services—selling auto parts, providing consultations, even hosting workshops."

Junior's eyes widened. "So that's how we started making more money without working extra hours!"

"Exactly. By diversifying services, we increased our earnings without necessarily increasing di workload," Marcus confirmed.

Keisha pondered aloud, "But what if we don't own a business? How can we apply this?"

"Whether yuh employed or not, think 'bout side hustles. Skills like baking, sewing, tutoring—use dem to earn extra income," Selene suggested.

Jasmine interjected, "Also, consider digital platforms. Freelancing online can tap into a global market."

Marcus emphasized, "But be wise with your time. Focus on high-impact activities that offer di best return for your effort."

The Power of Compound Efforts

Uncle Roy joined the discussion, his presence commanding respectful silence.

"Yuh know, small earnings add up over time. Just like how every drop fills di bucket," he began. "If yuh save and invest consistently, even small amounts can grow significantly."

Marcus seized the moment to introduce a new concept. "This brings us to di idea of compound efforts. Not just compound interest, but how consistently applying ourselves multiplies results."

Keisha nodded thoughtfully. "So, it's not just one big action, but many small ones combined."

"Exactly," Marcus affirmed. "And when yuh earn more, avoid lifestyle inflation. Don't increase your spending just because yuh making more."

Junior laughed sheepishly. "Guilty as charged!"

The group chuckled, but the lesson was clear.

Financial Lessons and Practical Takeaways

1. **Understand Your Worth**
   a. **Action:** Assess your skills and determine how to monetize them effectively.
   b. **Takeaway:** Don't undervalue your talents; they are keys to increasing your earnings.
2. **Diversify Income Streams**
   a. **Action:** Explore side hustles or additional services you can offer.
   b. **Takeaway:** Multiple income sources provide financial stability and growth opportunities.
3. **Invest in Yourself**
   a. **Action:** Pursue education and skill development.
   b. **Takeaway:** Enhancing your abilities increases your earning potential over time.
4. **Practice Smart Spending**
   a. **Action:** Avoid unnecessary expenses, especially as your income grows.
   b. **Takeaway:** Saving enhances earnings; money not spent is money preserved.

5. **Implement Compound Efforts**
    a. **Action:** Consistently work towards your financial goals through small, regular actions.
    b. **Takeaway:** Small efforts accumulate, leading to significant results over time.

Scene 6: Bridging to the Next Chapter

As the meeting wrapped up, Marcus looked around at the attentive faces.

"Remember, earning is just one part of di equation. Managing and growing that money is equally important," he emphasized.

Selene smiled. "Which means our next focus should be on budgeting and making our money stretch further."

Jasmine winked. "Budgeting like a boss!"

Uncle Roy raised his glass of sorrel. "To wisdom gained and applied. Di journey continues."

Marcus raised his own glass. "To taking control of our financial destinies."

Setting Up Future Books

As the team dispersed, Marcus pulled Jasmine aside.

"Been thinking 'bout compiling these lessons into a guide. Maybe even a series," he mused.

Her eyes lit up. "That's a brilliant idea! We could call it 'Money Mek Wi Talk.' Start with basics and then delve deeper."

He nodded. "Yes. And perhaps the next volume can focus on 'Investment 101.' Teach people how to make their money work for them."

"People are hungry for this knowledge, especially presented in a way that resonates with them culturally," Jasmine agreed.

"Then it's settled. Let's start planning," Marcus decided.

Thoughts

Marcus stood once more on his balcony that evening, the stars flickering like diamonds against the velvet sky. Selene joined him, resting her head on his shoulder.

"Proud of you," she whispered.

He wrapped an arm around her. "Couldn't have done it without you. But there's so much more to do. So many lives to touch."

She smiled. "One step at a time. Tonight, we rest. Tomorrow, we continue building."

He gazed into the distance, a sense of purpose filling his heart. "Yes. Tomorrow, we continue."

Stay tuned for Chapter 11: Budgeting Like a Boss—Making Money Stretch

Chapter 11: Budgeting Like a Boss—Making Money Stretch

The Money Just A Disappear

The evening sky painted hues of orange and pink over Kingston as Marcus sat hunched over the dining table, surrounded by a sea of crumpled receipts and bank statements. The oscillating fan did little to cool the beads of sweat forming on his brow.

"Selene! Come check dis out!" he called, frustration evident in his voice.

Selene emerged from the kitchen, wiping her hands on a dish towel. "What happen now, Marcus?" she asked, concern etched on her face.

He ran a hand over his short-cropped hair. "Mi cyaan understand how di money dem just a vanish. Wi making decent earnings, but by di end of di month, di account dry like drought."

She glanced over the scattered papers. "Hmm, is like water through basket. Wi need fi find di leak."

He sighed heavily. "Mi feel like mi working so hard, but mi nuh see di fruits of mi labor. Something haffi give."

Selene placed a reassuring hand on his shoulder. "Maybe it's time wi build a proper budget. Without one, wi just a sail without compass."

Marcus frowned. "Budgeting always sound so restricting to mi. Mi nuh want fi feel like mi cyaa enjoy di money mi work hard for."

She smiled gently. "Is not about restriction, love. Is about control. If yuh nuh direct yuh money, it will direct you."

He looked into her eyes, the weight of her words sinking in. "Yuh right. Wi need fi take charge."

Uncle Roy's Golden Rule

The next afternoon found Marcus and Selene on Uncle Roy's breezy veranda, the aroma of jerk chicken wafting through the air. Birds chirped in the mango tree overhead as the old man rocked slowly in his chair.

"Uncle Roy, wi come fi some advice," Marcus began.

He chuckled. "Ah, mi wonder when unuh would reach out. Di way yuh face set, mi know is money matters."

Selene nodded. "Is like di money just a fly out wi hands. Wi cyaa seem fi hold on to it."

Uncle Roy sipped his lemongrass tea thoughtfully. "Well, yuh ever hear di saying, 'If yuh fail fi plan, yuh plan fi fail'?"

Marcus nodded slowly.

"Budgeting is that plan. It nuh matter how much money yuh make; if yuh nuh manage it properly, it will disappear like morning dew," Uncle Roy continued.

"But Uncle Roy, mi always feel like budgeting mean mi haffi give up everything mi enjoy," Marcus admitted.

He shook his head. "Not so, Marcus. Budgeting nuh mean deprivation. It mean discipline. Is like planting a garden—you haffi nurture it fi reap di harvest."

Selene leaned forward. "So how we start? What's di first step?"

Uncle Roy smiled. "First, yuh haffi know where every dollar a go. Track yuh spending fi a month. Den, yuh categorize needs versus wants."

"Needs versus wants," Marcus repeated thoughtfully.

"Yes. Food, shelter, basic utilities—dem are needs. Eating out every week, new gadgets—dem are wants. Once yuh differentiate, yuh can adjust accordingly," Uncle Roy explained.

Setting Up the Budget

Back home, Marcus and Selene transformed the dining table into their budgeting headquarters. Selene opened her laptop, pulling up a spreadsheet.

"Alright, let's start with income," she said.

Marcus listed:

Income:

- **Marcus's Garage Earnings:** J$300,000
- **Selene's Salary:** J$120,000
- **Side Projects:** J$50,000

Total Income: J$470,000

"Now, expenses," Selene prompted.

They began detailing every cost:

Expenses:

- **Mortgage:** J$80,000
- **Utilities:** J$25,000
- **Car Loan:** J$40,000
- **Groceries:** J$60,000

- **Transportation:** J$20,000
- **Insurance:** J$15,000
- **Eating Out:** J$50,000
- **Entertainment:** J$15,000
- **Clothing:** J$10,000
- **Miscellaneous:** J$20,000

Total Expenses: J$335,000

"Wait, so we should have J$135,000 left over each month?" Marcus asked, perplexed.

"But wi nuh see dat money, so where it a go?" Selene questioned.

They dug deeper, realizing untracked cash withdrawals and small daily purchases were adding up.

"Di likkle $500 here and dere fi snacks, di random online shopping—it all adds up," Selene noted.

Marcus shook his head. "No wonder di money a slip through wi fingers."

Scene 4: Cutting Costs and Smart Spending

"Alright, time fi make adjustments," Selene declared.

They revisited each expense:

1. **Eating Out (J$50,000):**
   a. **Action:** Cut down to dining out once a week.
   b. **New Budget:** J$20,000
   c. **Savings:** J$30,000
2. **Groceries (J$60,000):**
   a. **Action:** Shop with a list, buy in bulk, utilize local markets.
   b. **New Budget:** J$50,000

    c.   **Savings:** J$10,000
3. **Utilities (J$25,000):**
   a.   **Action:** Unplug devices, switch to energy-efficient bulbs, limit AC use.
   b.   **New Budget:** J$20,000
   c.   **Savings:** J$5,000
4. **Entertainment & Miscellaneous (J$35,000):**
   a.   **Action:** Opt for free or low-cost activities, set a strict limit.
   b.   **New Budget:** J$20,000
   c.   **Savings:** J$15,000

Total Monthly Savings: J$60,000

"Wi just freed up an extra J$60,000 per month!" Selene exclaimed.

Marcus grinned. "Dat's significant. Wi can boost our savings and start investing fi true."

Setting Financial Goals

"Now that we have more available funds, let's assign them wisely," Selene suggested.

They decided to:

- **Emergency Fund:** Allocate J$30,000/month until they reach six months' worth of expenses.
- **Investment Portfolio:** Allocate J$20,000/month into stocks and bonds.
- **Education Fund:** Allocate J$10,000/month towards courses and workshops.

Marcus looked satisfied. "Now we're not just earning money—we're making it work for us."

Marcus's Mini Challenge

Marcus had an idea. "You know, wi should challenge ourselves and di readers."

Selene raised an eyebrow playfully. "Oh? What's on your mind?"

"Let's do a one-month budgeting challenge. Track every spend, stick to di budget, and see how much we save. Encourage others fi do di same," he proposed.

She clapped her hands. "I love it! And we can share tips and motivate each other along di way."

Overcoming Temptations

During the challenge, temptations arose.

"Marcus, a new restaurant open up downtown. Everybody talking 'bout it," Junior mentioned at work.

Marcus felt the allure but remembered his goal. "Sound good, but mi sticking to mi budget dis month. Maybe next time."

Similarly, Selene's friends invited her to a weekend getaway.

"Mi would love to, but mi haffi pass dis time," she told them, standing firm.

Reaping the Rewards

At the end of the month, they reviewed their progress.

"Marcus, wi saved an additional J$70,000 dis month!" Selene announced excitedly.

He beamed. "Wi did it! Budgeting really give wi control and peace of mind."

They decided to celebrate modestly with a homemade dinner and a movie at home.

Uncle Roy stopped by, a proud smile on his face. "Mi hear unuh a budget like champions!"

Marcus laughed. "All thanks to your wisdom, Uncle Roy."

Financial Lessons and Practical Takeaways

1. **Track Every Dollar**
   a. **Action:** Use apps or a notebook to record all expenses daily.
   b. **Takeaway:** Awareness prevents money from slipping away unnoticed.
2. **Differentiate Between Needs and Wants**
   a. **Action:** List expenses and categorize them honestly.
   b. **Takeaway:** Prioritizing needs over wants curbs unnecessary spending.
3. **Set Clear Financial Goals**
   a. **Action:** Define what you want to achieve financially (e.g., savings amount, debt payoff).
   b. **Takeaway:** Goals provide direction and motivation to stick to the budget.
4. **Make Adjustments**
   a. **Action:** Find cost-effective alternatives without sacrificing quality of life.
   b. **Takeaway:** Small changes lead to significant savings over time.
5. **Stay Committed**
   a. **Action:** Resist temptations that derail your financial plans.

b. **Takeaway:** Discipline is key to achieving financial stability.

Mini Budgeting Challenge for Readers

Challenge: For the next 30 days, track every expense, create a budget, and identify areas to cut costs.

Steps:

1. **List Your Income and Expenses**
   a. Write down all sources of income.
   b. List all fixed and variable expenses.
2. **Set Financial Goals**
   a. Decide how much you want to save or allocate towards debts.
3. **Identify Cutbacks**
   a. Find at least three areas where you can reduce spending.
4. **Monitor Daily**
   a. Keep a daily log of expenses to stay on track.
5. **Review Weekly**
   a. Assess your progress and make necessary adjustments.

Outcome: Experience the empowerment of budgeting and witness how much you can save in just one month!

Setting Up Future Books

One evening, as they relaxed after a long day, Marcus turned to Selene.

"Yuh know, mi thinking 'bout compiling all these experiences and lessons into a book series," he mused.

She smiled brightly. "I think that's a wonderful idea! 'Money Mek Wi Talk' could help so many people."

"Exactly. And maybe di next book can delve deeper into saving strategies and building that emergency fund," he suggested.

She nodded. "Yes! 'Saving for Di Future' sounds like a perfect next step."

Thoughts

Standing on the balcony, the cool night air wrapping around them, Marcus felt a sense of fulfillment.

"Budgeting nuh just help wi save money—it strengthen wi partnership," he observed.

Selene rested her head on his shoulder. "True. Wi working as a team towards a brighter future."

He kissed her forehead gently. "To many more victories together."

She raised her glass. "To us, and to making money work for wi."

Stay tuned for Chapter 12: Saving for Di Future—How to Build an Emergency Fund

Chapter 12: Saving for Di Future—How to Build an Emergency Fund

When Life Hit Yuh Hard

The sun blazed overhead as Marcus navigated the busy streets of Kingston, the scent of jerk chicken wafting through the open car windows. Selene sat beside him, humming along to the reggae tunes playing softly on the radio.

"Dis week been hectic, but wi finally get some time fi weself," Marcus smiled, turning the corner towards their favorite hillside spot.

"True. Mi can't wait fi just relax and enjoy di view," Selene agreed.

Suddenly, a loud bang shattered the tranquility. The car jerked violently, and Marcus struggled to control the steering wheel.

"Marcus! What was dat?" Selene exclaimed, gripping the seat.

He eased the car to the side of the road, heart pounding. "Mi nuh know, but it nuh sound good at all."

They stepped out to find smoke billowing from under the hood. A passing driver slowed down. "Everything alright, boss?"

"Engine problem, it seem so," Marcus replied, frustration creeping in.

After arranging a tow to the nearest mechanic, they received the grim news.

"The engine mash up, boss. Yuh looking at about J$150,000 fi fix it," the mechanic stated.

Marcus felt his stomach drop. "J$150,000? Mi never plan fi dis expense."

Selene sighed, placing a hand on his arm. "What wi going do now?"

He shook his head. "Mi nuh sure. Dis a go set us back big time."

Uncle Roy's Lesson on "Rainy Day Money"

That evening, they sat in Uncle Roy's cozy living room, the aroma of fresh cocoa tea filling the air.

"Uncle Roy, di car engine blow, and di repair cost high," Marcus confessed, his shoulders slumped.

"Lawd have mercy. Dat rough, mi youth," Uncle Roy replied sympathetically.

"Wi nuh have di extra funds fi cover it without dipping into di money fi bills," Selene added.

Uncle Roy nodded knowingly. "Dis is why mi always seh, 'Save fi di rainy day before di storm come.' Life full a unexpected turns."

"Wi been trying fi manage wi spending, but savings nuh build up enough yet," Marcus admitted.

"Is not too late fi start. An emergency fund is like a cushion fi soften di blows life throw at yuh. Di key is fi start small but be consistent," Uncle Roy advised.

"How much wi should aim fi save?" Selene inquired.

"Ideally, three to six months of expenses. But begin wid what yuh can. Even a small amount can mek a big difference when trouble come," he explained.

How Fi Build an Emergency Fund

Determined to take action, Marcus and Selene sat down the next day to map out a plan.

"Wi need fi figure out how fi save up at least J$200,000 over di next few months," Marcus stated.

Selene tapped her pen thoughtfully. "First, let's set up an automatic transfer from our paychecks into a separate savings account each month."

"Good idea. If wi nuh see di money, wi less likely fi spend it," he agreed.

They decided on practical strategies:

1. **Automatic Transfers**
   a. Set up J$20,000 monthly automatic transfer to savings.
2. **No-Spend Weeks**
   a. Designate one week per month where they spend only on necessities.
3. **Cutting Non-Essential Expenses**
   a. Reduce dining out and entertainment to save an extra J$10,000 monthly.
4. **Selling Unused Items**
   a. Sell gently used clothing and electronics online for additional income.
5. **Extra Income Opportunities**
   a. Marcus would take on additional small repair jobs; Selene would offer weekend tutoring.

Challenges of Saving & How to Overcome Dem

As the weeks passed, they faced temptations and challenges.

"Marcus, di new smartphone release today. Mi phone acting up; maybe mi should get it," Selene mentioned one afternoon.

He looked up, considering. "Mi understand, but remember di goal. Can it wait until wi reach our savings target?"

She sighed. "Yuh right. Mi can manage a likkle longer."

Another time, Marcus was invited to a weekend getaway with friends.

"Mi could use di break," he thought aloud.

Selene raised an eyebrow. "And spend di money wi saving fi di car? Priorities, love."

He chuckled. "True. Wi haffi stay focused."

They kept each other accountable, resisting impulses and reminding themselves of the bigger picture.

Marcus & Selene's 6-Month Savings Plan

They mapped out a realistic plan:

Monthly Savings Breakdown

- **Automatic Savings:** J$20,000
- **Reduced Expenses:** J$10,000
- **Extra Income:** J$15,000 (Marcus's repairs: J$10,000; Selene's tutoring: J$5,000)

- **Total Monthly Savings:** J$45,000

6-Month Total Savings: J$270,000

"This way, wi not only cover di car repair but also have extra fi di emergency fund," Selene smiled.

"Exactly. And if wi continue, wi can build up di recommended six months' expenses," Marcus added.

Mini Savings Challenge for Readers

Challenge: Save J$10,000 in 30 Days

Step-by-Step Guide

1. **Set Up Automatic Savings**
   a. **Action:** Arrange with your bank fi transfer J$2,500 weekly into a savings account.
   b. **Benefit:** Consistent saving without thinking about it.
2. **Implement a No-Spend Week**
   a. **Action:** Choose one week to spend only on essentials.
   b. **Benefit:** Save approximately J$3,000 by avoiding unnecessary purchases.
3. **Cut One Regular Expense**
   a. **Action:** Skip buying lunch; bring food from home.
   b. **Benefit:** Save J$2,000 over a month.
4. **Earn Extra Income**
   a. **Action:** Offer a service (e.g., washing cars, babysitting) or sell items you no longer need.
   b. **Benefit:** Earn an additional J$2,500.

Total Savings in 30 Days: J$10,000

Encouragement: Small actions add up. Challenge yourself and watch your savings grow!

Bridge to Next Chapter

One evening, as they reviewed their progress, Marcus turned to Selene.

"Mi proud of how far wi come. Saving nuh easy, but wi mek it work," he said.

She nodded. "And now, wi can handle emergencies without panic."

"Yuh know, with dis discipline, wi can start thinking 'bout investing next," Marcus mused.

Selene's eyes sparkled. "Yes! Mek wi money work fi wi."

He smiled. "Time fi explore di world of investments and grow wi wealth further."

Financial Lessons and Practical Takeaways

1. **Expect the Unexpected**
   a. **Action:** Start an emergency fund to prepare for unforeseen expenses.
   b. **Takeaway:** Financial security reduces stress when life throws curveballs.
2. **Start Small but Be Consistent**
   a. **Action:** Save a manageable amount regularly.
   b. **Takeaway:** Consistency builds substantial savings over time.
3. **Prioritize Needs Over Wants**
   a. **Action:** Delay non-essential purchases.
   b. **Takeaway:** Sacrifices now lead to greater benefits later.
4. **Find Creative Ways to Save and Earn**
   a. **Action:** Reduce expenses and seek additional income sources.

b. **Takeaway:** Increasing the gap between income and expenses accelerates savings.

5. **Accountability Partners Help**
    a. **Action:** Work with someone to stay on track.
    b. **Takeaway:** Mutual support enhances commitment to financial goals.

Thoughts

Building an emergency fund empowered Marcus and Selene to face life's uncertainties with confidence. Their journey illustrates that saving is not just about money—it's about building a foundation for a secure future.

Stay tuned for Chapter 13: Cash Flow Control—How to Manage Yuh Money Properly

Chapter 13: Cash Flow Control— How to Manage Yuh Money Properly

"Why Di Money Always Done Quick?"

Marcus leaned back in his chair at the dining table, eyebrows knitted in frustration as he stared at his laptop screen. Bank statements and bills were scattered around him. Selene entered the room, noticing his distress.

"Marcus, yuh alright?" she asked gently.

He sighed heavily. "Selene, mi nuh understand how, after all di budgeting and saving, di money still a finish before month-end. Is like as soon as wi get paid, it disappear."

She pulled up a chair beside him. "Let mi see what gwan."

"Look yah," he pointed at the screen. "Wi pay di bills, put money inna di savings, but mi still feel strapped fi cash halfway through di month."

Selene nodded thoughtfully. "Maybe is a cash flow problem. Budgeting show wi di big picture, but cash flow is about timing—when money come in and when it go out."

"Yuh have a point. Mi get paid from di garage at irregular times, and some clients delay payment," Marcus realized.

She smiled. "Exactly. If wi nuh manage di flow properly, wi can run short even if wi earning enough overall."

Uncle Roy's Lesson on "Di Money River"

Determined to find a solution, Marcus and Selene visited Uncle Roy the next day. They found him tending to his garden, humming a familiar tune.

"Uncle Roy, wi need fi pick yuh brain 'bout something," Marcus said, walking up the path.

He looked up, a warm smile on his face. "Ah, Marcus and Selene! Come siddung pon di veranda."

After they explained their predicament, Uncle Roy leaned back in his rocking chair. "Cash flow is like a river, mi youth. If di river block upstream, downstream suffer. Yuh haffi ensure dat di inflow and outflow balance out."

"So even if wi earning enough, bad timing can mek wi short?" Selene asked.

"Exactly. Yuh need fi track when money come in and when it due fi go out. Sometime, adjusting di dates can mek a big difference," he advised.

Marcus rubbed his chin. "But how wi manage dat, Uncle Roy?"

He chuckled softly. "Mi show unuh a simple method. Write down all yuh expected income and expenses along di calendar dates. Dat way, yuh can foresee any gaps and plan accordingly."

"Di Cash Flow System"

Back home, Marcus and Selene sat at the kitchen table with a large calendar spread before them.

"Alright, let's list all di income sources and when dem come in," Selene suggested.

Income:

- **Marcus's Garage Earnings:** Variable dates, usually weekly.
- **Selene's Salary:** 25th of each month.
- **Side Projects:** Irregular dates.

"Now, list di fixed expenses and due dates," Marcus added.

Expenses:

- **Mortgage:** 1st of the month.
- **Utilities:** Between 5th and 10th.
- **Car Loan:** 15th.
- **Insurance:** 20th.

"Mi see di problem," Selene pointed out. "Most of di big bills due before mi salary come in."

"True, and some months, clients delay payments, so di garage money unpredictable," Marcus acknowledged.

"Wi need fi align di expenses wid di income," she suggested.

"Maybe wi can negotiate wid di bank fi adjust di mortgage payment date," he proposed.

Selene nodded. "Worth a try. Also, set up a buffer account fi hold extra funds when income higher, fi cover times when it's lower."

"And for clients, mi can implement a more structured payment schedule or offer incentives fi early payment," Marcus considered.

Preventing Shortfalls & Avoiding Paycheck-to-Paycheck Living

Over the next few days, they took proactive steps:

1. **Adjusted Bill Dates:**
    - Contacted service providers to change due dates closer to when income arrives.
2. **Established a Cash Buffer:**
    - Set aside a month's worth of expenses in a separate account to cover any timing gaps.
3. **Structured Client Payments:**
    - Implemented contracts with clear payment terms.
    - Offered a 5% discount for clients who paid upfront or on delivery.
4. **Monitored Cash Flow Regularly:**
    - Used a spreadsheet to track cash inflows and outflows weekly.

One afternoon, Marcus met with Jasmine at a café to discuss business.

"Jasmine, mi realize dat managing cash flow is as important as making sales," he shared.

She grinned. "Definitely! Cash flow management can mek or break a business. Proud of you fi taking it seriously."

"Is not easy, but mi determined fi avoid living paycheck to paycheck," he affirmed.

Marcus & Selene's Monthly Money Flow Plan

They formalized their plan:

1. **Create a Cash Flow Calendar:**
    a. **Week 1:**
        i. **Income:** Expected garage payments.
        ii. **Expenses:** Mortgage payment.
    b. **Week 2:**
        i. **Income:** Selene's tutoring payments.

ii.   **Expenses:** Utilities. (And so on for each week.)

2. **Maintain a Minimum Balance:**
   a. Keep at least J$50,000 in the checking account at all times.
3. **Automate Essential Payments:**
   a. Set up automatic bill payments to avoid late fees.
4. **Review Weekly:**
   a. Allocate time every Sunday to review the upcoming week's cash flow.

"With dis system, wi can foresee any potential shortfalls and adjust accordingly," Selene stated confidently.

Marcus smiled. "Peace of mind at last."

Mini Cash Flow Challenge for Readers

Challenge: Take Control of Yuh Money in 30 Days

Step-by-Step Guide

1. **Map Out Your Income and Expenses:**
   a. **Action:** Use a calendar to note when you receive income and when bills are due.
   b. **Benefit:** Visualize cash flow gaps and surpluses.
2. **Adjust Payment Dates:**
   a. **Action:** Contact service providers to change bill due dates to align with income.
   b. **Benefit:** Prevents periods of cash shortage.
3. **Build a Cash Cushion:**
   a. **Action:** Aim to save enough to cover one month's expenses in a buffer account.
   b. **Benefit:** Provides a safety net for unexpected delays.
4. **Monitor Cash Flow Weekly:**
   a. **Action:** Review inflows and outflows every week.

b.   **Benefit:** Stay proactive in managing finances.
5.   **Communicate with Creditors:**
      a.   **Action:** If cash flow is tight, talk to creditors about flexible payment options.
      b.   **Benefit:** Avoids missed payments and maintains good relationships.

Outcome: Achieve smoother cash flow and reduce financial stress within a month!

Bridge to Next Chapter

One evening, as they relaxed on the porch, Marcus shared his thoughts with Selene.

"Now that wi have di cash flow under control, mi feel more confident 'bout taking di next steps in our financial journey," he said.

She looked at him curiously. "What you thinking 'bout?"

"Well, wi covered budgeting, saving, and managing money properly. But wi need fi understand di dangers out there—like bad debt," he explained.

Selene nodded. "True. Avoiding money traps is crucial."

"Exactly. Wi haffi be wise 'bout how wi handle credit and loans," Marcus agreed.

"Then let's dive into that next," she smiled.

Financial Lessons and Practical Takeaways

1.   **Understand Cash Flow Timing**
      a.   **Action:** Align bill payments with income dates.

b. **Takeaway:** Prevents cash shortages even when earning enough overall.

2. **Create a Cash Buffer**
   a. **Action:** Save a minimum balance to cover at least one month's expenses.
   b. **Takeaway:** Provides a cushion against income delays or unexpected costs.
3. **Automate and Monitor**
   a. **Action:** Set up automatic payments and review cash flow weekly.
   b. **Takeaway:** Reduces the risk of late fees and keeps you informed.
4. **Communicate and Negotiate**
   a. **Action:** Engage with creditors or clients to adjust payment terms when necessary.
   b. **Takeaway:** Flexibility can ease cash flow pressures and build stronger relationships.
5. **Plan for Irregular Income**
   a. **Action:** For variable earnings, base your budget on the lowest expected income.
   b. **Takeaway:** Ensures expenses are always covered, and surplus can bolster savings.

Thoughts

By mastering cash flow control, Marcus and Selene unlocked a new level of financial stability. Their proactive approach allowed them to manage their resources effectively, setting the stage for wise investment decisions and long-term wealth building.

Stay tuned for Chapter 14: Avoiding Money Traps—Understanding Bad Debt

Chapter 14: Avoiding Money Traps—Understanding Bad Debt

"Di Credit Card Trap"

The midday sun blazed over Kingston, casting sharp shadows on the bustling sidewalks. Marcus wiped the sweat from his brow as he locked up the garage for lunch. Just then, he spotted Junior sitting on a nearby bench, his usually bright demeanor clouded with worry.

"Junior! Wha gwaan, mi youth? Yuh good?" Marcus called out, approaching him.

Junior looked up, a forced smile on his face. "Hey, Marcus. Mi alright."

Marcus wasn't convinced. "Yuh sure? Yuh look like something a bother yuh."

Junior hesitated before sighing heavily. "Is just... mi in a little financial bind."

Marcus sat beside him. "Talk to mi. Maybe mi can help."

Junior glanced around before lowering his voice. "Mi get caught up wid di credit card, Marcus. Di debt piling up, and di interest killing mi. Every month, mi pay, but it nuh seem fi go down."

Marcus frowned. "How come yuh reach deh so?"

Junior rubbed his hands together nervously. "Well, couple months back, mi needed a new phone. Mi couldn't afford it cash, so mi use di credit card. Den some unexpected expenses come up, and mi use it again. Before mi know it, di balance high, and mi cyaa manage di payments."

"Mi understand. Di convenience can be a trap," Marcus nodded. "But yuh haffi face it head-on."

Junior looked defeated. "Mi just feel overwhelmed. Di minimum payments nah mek a dent, and mi afraid fi tell mi family."

"Yuh nuh alone in dis, Junior. Plenty people get caught in di same situation. Let's see how wi can tackle it together," Marcus assured him.

Uncle Roy's Wisdom—"Good Debt vs. Bad Debt"

Later that day, Marcus and Junior made their way to Uncle Roy's place. The old man was sitting on his veranda, the scent of freshly brewed ginger tea wafting through the air.

"Uncle Roy, wi need yuh wisdom," Marcus greeted him.

He looked up with a gentle smile. "Always good fi see unuh. Come, siddung."

Junior shuffled his feet. "Uncle Roy, mi inna problem wid credit card debt. Di interest a drown mi."

Uncle Roy nodded knowingly. "Ah, di credit card—a double-edged sword. Convenient, but dangerous if nuh managed properly."

"Mi didn't realize how quickly di debt could spiral," Junior admitted.

"Let mi tell unuh 'bout good debt versus bad debt," Uncle Roy began. "Good debt is when yuh borrow fi invest in something dat will bring returns—like education or a business. Bad debt is borrowing fi tings dat depreciate or nuh necessary, like expensive gadgets or lavish spending."

Marcus chimed in, "So using credit fi buy tings dat nuh add value to yuh life is bad debt."

"Exactly," Uncle Roy affirmed. "Credit cards charge high interest. If yuh only pay di minimum, yuh end up paying much more over time."

Junior sighed. "Mi see dat now."

"But all is not lost. Di important ting is fi recognize di mistake and make a plan fi get out," Uncle Roy encouraged.

"How Fi Get Outta Debt"

Back at Marcus's home, he, Selene, and Junior gathered around the kitchen table.

"First step is to know exactly how much yuh owe," Selene said, pulling out a notebook.

Junior handed over his statements. "Di total balance is J$200,000, and di interest rate is 40% per annum."

Marcus whistled softly. "Dat high, but wi can work wid it."

"Alright, here's what wi can do," Selene began outlining:

1. **Stop Using Di Credit Card**
   a. **Action:** Cut up the card to avoid accumulating more debt.
   b. **Junior:** "Mi will do dat. No more swiping."
2. **Create a Debt Repayment Plan**
   a. **Action:** Calculate a fixed amount to pay each month that's more than the minimum.
   b. **Marcus:** "If yuh pay J$20,000 monthly, yuh can clear di debt in about 12 months."
3. **Negotiate with Di Bank**
   a. **Action:** Request a lower interest rate or a consolidation loan with better terms.

b. **Junior:** "Mi never think 'bout dat. Mi will set an appointment."

4. **Increase Income Streams**
   a. **Action:** Take on extra work or side jobs to boost income.
   b. **Junior:** "Mi can offer after-hours mechanic work or help mi uncle on weekends."

5. **Cut Unnecessary Expenses**
   a. **Action:** Reduce spending to free up more money for debt repayment.
   b. **Junior:** "Mi will limit eating out and unnecessary purchases."

"Remember, discipline is key," Selene emphasized. "It might be tough, but it's worth it."

"Thanks, guys. Mi feel more hopeful now," Junior smiled gratefully.

"Di Money Trap Checklist"

Marcus decided to share some common money traps with Junior and others.

Money Traps to Avoid:

1. **High-Interest Credit Cards**
   a. **Trap:** Tempting to use but hard to pay off due to high interest.
   b. **Avoid:** Use cash or debit cards; if using credit, pay off in full monthly.

2. **Payday Loans**
   a. **Trap:** Quick cash with extremely high fees and interest.
   b. **Avoid:** Build an emergency fund to cover unexpected expenses.

3. **Rent-to-Own Schemes**

    a.   **Trap:** End up paying far more than the item's value.

    b.   **Avoid:** Save up and buy outright when possible.

4. **Get-Rich-Quick Investments**

    a.   **Trap:** Promises of high returns with low risk—often scams.

    b.   **Avoid:** Research thoroughly; if it sounds too good to be true, it probably is.

5. **Over-Reliance on Credit**

    a.   **Trap:** Using credit for daily expenses leads to debt accumulation.

    b.   **Avoid:** Stick to a budget; use credit wisely.

"Knowledge is power," Marcus declared. "When yuh know di traps, yuh can sidestep dem."

Mini "Debt-Free Challenge" for Readers

Challenge: Escape Bad Debt in 30 Days

Step-by-Step Guide

1. **List All Debts**

    a.   **Action:** Write down all debts, interest rates, and minimum payments.

    b.   **Benefit:** Clear understanding of what you owe.

2. **Prioritize Debts**

    a.   **Action:** Focus on paying off debts with the highest interest rates first.

    b.   **Benefit:** Saves money on interest over time.

3. **Create a Repayment Plan**

    a.   **Action:** Determine how much extra you can pay each month.

    b.   **Benefit:** Accelerates debt elimination.

4. **Negotiate with Creditors**

a. **Action:** Contact lenders to discuss lower interest rates or payment plans.

b. **Benefit:** Potentially reduces the total amount owed.

5. **Increase Income**

a. **Action:** Explore side gigs or sell unused items.

b. **Benefit:** More funds to allocate toward debt.

6. **Avoid New Debt**

a. **Action:** Refrain from using credit cards or taking new loans.

b. **Benefit:** Prevents worsening the situation.

7. **Stay Accountable**

a. **Action:** Share your goals with a trusted friend or family member.

b. **Benefit:** Encouragement and support to stay on track.

Outcome: Begin the journey to becoming debt-free and gain financial freedom!

Bridge to Next Chapter

A few weeks later, Junior met up with Marcus and Selene, a renewed energy about him.

"Guess what? Mi paid off one of mi smaller debts already, and di big one is reducing," Junior beamed.

"Dat's fantastic news!" Selene exclaimed.

"See what discipline and a plan can achieve?" Marcus grinned.

"Mi couldn't have done it without unuh help," Junior said sincerely.

"Now that you're getting out of debt, it's a perfect time fi start thinking 'bout how to use debt wisely," Marcus suggested.

"Yuh mean there's such a ting as good debt?" Junior asked, intrigued.

Uncle Roy, who had just joined them, smiled. "Ah, that's a conversation for another day. But yes, debt can be a tool fi build wealth if used properly."

Selene nodded. "Exactly. Next, wi can explore how to leverage debt fi invest and grow."

"Looking forward to learning more," Junior said enthusiastically.

Financial Lessons and Practical Takeaways

1. **Understand the Difference Between Good and Bad Debt**
    a. **Action:** Recognize that not all debt is harmful; some can help build wealth.
    b. **Takeaway:** Use debt strategically for investments, not consumption.
2. **Avoid High-Interest Debt**
    a. **Action:** Steer clear of credit cards and loans with exorbitant interest rates.
    b. **Takeaway:** High-interest debt can trap you in a cycle that's hard to escape.
3. **Create a Debt Repayment Plan**
    a. **Action:** Prioritize debts, negotiate with creditors, and pay more than the minimum.
    b. **Takeaway:** A structured plan accelerates debt elimination.
4. **Increase Income and Reduce Expenses**
    a. **Action:** Find additional income sources and cut unnecessary spending.
    b. **Takeaway:** Freeing up cash helps pay down debt faster.
5. **Stay Disciplined and Seek Support**
    a. **Action:** Commit to your plan and lean on others for help.
    b. **Takeaway:** Accountability boosts your chances of success.

Thoughts

Understanding and avoiding bad debt is a crucial step toward financial empowerment. Marcus, Selene, and Junior's journey highlights the importance of awareness, discipline, and proactive strategies in overcoming financial challenges.

Stay tuned for Chapter 15: Smart Borrowing—How to Use Debt to Build Wealth

Chapter 15: Smart Borrowing—How to Use Debt to Build Wealth

"Di Investment Loan Decision"

The late afternoon sun cast a warm glow over the garage as Marcus finished up the day's work. Wiping his hands on a rag, he gazed thoughtfully at the empty lot next door. The idea of expanding his business had been on his mind for weeks, but uncertainty lingered.

Selene pulled up in her car, stepping out with a bright smile. "Hey, love! Yuh look deep in thought."

He smiled back. "Hey, Selene. Just thinking 'bout di possibilities. If wi could acquire dat lot, wi could double di size of di garage, offer more services."

She raised an eyebrow. "So what's holding yuh back?"

Marcus sighed. "Mi nuh sure if mi ready fi take on a loan fi finance it. After seeing how Junior struggle wid debt, mi hesitant."

Selene touched his arm gently. "But remember, not all debt is bad. If used wisely, it can help us grow."

He nodded slowly. "True, but mi still have mi doubts."

Just then, Jasmine arrived, carrying a folder under her arm. "Hey, team! Got some exciting ideas to share."

Marcus chuckled. "Perfect timing. Wi need all di advice wi can get."

Uncle Roy's Wisdom—"How Fi Use Debt Wisely"

Later that evening, Marcus and Selene visited Uncle Roy, hoping to gain clarity.

"Uncle Roy, mi thinking 'bout expanding di garage, but it would mean taking out a business loan," Marcus began.

Uncle Roy gazed at him thoughtfully. "Ah, so yuh considering leveraging debt fi grow?"

"Yes, but mi afraid of ending up in bad debt," Marcus admitted.

Uncle Roy leaned forward. "Listen, Marcus. Debt itself nuh bad or good. Is how yuh use it. Good debt is like a tool—it can help yuh build wealth if used properly. Bad debt drains yuh resources."

Selene nodded. "So what's di difference between investment debt and consumer debt?"

"Investment debt is borrowing fi tings dat appreciate in value or generate income—like business expansion, real estate, or education. Consumer debt is for tings dat lose value—like fancy cars or unnecessary gadgets," Uncle Roy explained.

Marcus considered this. "So taking a loan fi expand di garage could be good debt if it leads to higher profits."

"Exactly. But yuh haffi do yuh homework. Ensure di potential returns outweigh di costs," Uncle Roy advised.

He added, "And be careful of predatory lenders—loan sharks and high-interest schemes dat seem too good to be true but trap yuh in a cycle of debt."

"Mi hear bout dem. Mi will stick to reputable financial institutions,"
Marcus assured him.

"Good. Always read di fine print and ask questions," Uncle Roy
cautioned.

"Marcus Visits the Bank"

The next day, Marcus and Selene made their way to the Bank of
Jamaica, the cool air-conditioning a welcome relief from the midday
heat.

A friendly loan officer greeted them. "Good afternoon, Mr. Thomas, Ms.
Williams. How can I assist you today?"

Marcus shook his hand. "Mi interested in a business expansion loan fi
acquire di lot next door and expand mi garage."

"Certainly. Let's discuss your options," the loan officer replied, guiding
them to his office.

They sat down, and the loan officer pulled up some information on his
computer. "We offer several loan products for small businesses. Here's
one with a 10% interest rate over five years."

Marcus leaned in. "Are there any penalties for early repayment?"

"No penalties. In fact, we encourage early repayment," the officer
smiled.

Selene interjected. "What about di possibility of a lower interest rate?
We've been loyal customers for years and have a strong credit history."

The loan officer considered. "Given your excellent credit and business
performance, we could offer a rate of 8%."

Marcus's eyes lit up. "That would make a significant difference over di life of di loan."

"Absolutely. Every percentage point counts," the officer agreed.

"Are there any additional fees we should be aware of?" Selene asked.

"There's a processing fee of 1% of di loan amount, but I can request a waiver for half of that due to your longstanding relationship with the bank," he offered.

"Appreciate that," Marcus replied. "What kind of collateral are we looking at?"

"The collateral would typically be the property you're purchasing and any existing assets of the business," the loan officer explained.

Selene glanced at Marcus. "That seems reasonable."

Marcus nodded. "One more question. What support does the bank offer to businesses during di repayment period?"

"We provide financial advising services and can assist with cash flow management strategies to ensure your business thrives," the officer assured them.

"That's reassuring," Marcus said. "I think we're ready to move forward."

"Excellent. Let's begin the application process," the loan officer smiled.

"Warning on Predatory Lending"

Later that evening, as they recounted their experience to Uncle Roy, he nodded approvingly. "Glad yuh got favorable terms."

"Selene did a great job negotiating," Marcus grinned.

She shrugged modestly. "Always worth asking."

Uncle Roy's expression turned serious. "Just remember, not all lenders are so accommodating. Some prey on desperate borrowers, offering quick cash with hidden traps."

"Yuh mean like di loan sharks and those flashy quick-cash ads?" Marcus asked.

"Exactly. Dem lure people wid easy approvals but charge sky-high interest rates and harsh penalties. Before yuh know it, yuh owe twice or three times what yuh borrow," Uncle Roy warned.

Selene leaned forward. "But why would people go to dem?"

"Sometimes folks feel they have no other options, or they're swayed by di promise of fast money without checks," he explained. "But it's a dangerous path."

Marcus recalled, "Mi remember a story 'bout a man who borrowed from one of dem. When he couldn't pay back in time, they threatened his family."

"That's di reality. So always be cautious. Stick to reputable financial institutions, read di fine print, and never rush into agreements out of desperation," Uncle Roy advised.

"Sound advice, as always," Selene said gratefully.

Expanded "Borrow Wisely Challenge"

Challenge: How to Use Debt to Build Wealth in 30 Days

Mini Case Study:

Case 1: Lisa's Wise Investment

Lisa aspired to open a small bakery. She needed J$600,000 to secure a location, purchase equipment, and cover initial operating costs. She approached a reputable bank and secured a small business loan at 9% interest over five years.

Loan Details:

- **Loan Amount:** J$600,000
- **Interest Rate:** 9% per annum
- **Monthly Payment:** Approximately J$12,455
- **Total Repayment:** Approximately J$747,300

Outcome:

- **Monthly Revenue:** J$200,000
- **Monthly Expenses (including loan payment):** J$150,000
- **Profit After Expenses:** J$50,000

Lisa's bakery became popular, and her profits grew over time. She managed to repay the loan early, saving on interest, and eventually expanded her business further.

Case 2: David's Costly Mistake

David desired to live a luxurious lifestyle. He took out a personal loan of J$400,000 from a high-interest lender at 28% interest over four years to buy an expensive car.

Loan Details:

- **Loan Amount:** J$400,000
- **Interest Rate:** 28% per annum
- **Monthly Payment:** Approximately J$13,200
- **Total Repayment:** Approximately J$633,600

Outcome:

- **Depreciating Asset:** The car's value dropped significantly.
- **Financial Strain:** Loan payments consumed a large portion of his income.
- **Stress and Regret:** Struggled to keep up with payments, leading to financial and personal stress.

Conclusion:

- Lisa used debt to invest in a business that generated income.
- David used debt to purchase a depreciating asset that drained his finances.

Simple Loan Calculator Formula:

To assess if debt is worth it, calculate the Total Cost of the Loan and compare it to the Expected Return.

Monthly Payment Formula:

$$P = \frac{L \times r}{1 - (1 + r)^{-n}}$$

- P = Monthly payment
- L = Loan amount
- r = Monthly interest rate (annual rate divided by 12)
- n = Total number of payments (months)

Assessing the Loan:

1. **Calculate Monthly Payment (P).**
2. **Calculate Total Repayment:**

$$T = P \times n$$

3. **Estimate Total Earnings from Investment (E).**
4. **Determine Profit:**

$$\text{Profit} = E - T - \text{Other Expenses}$$

5. **If Profit is Positive and Sufficient, the Debt May Be Worthwhile.**

Step-by-Step Guide:

1. **Identify a Wealth-Building Opportunity**
   a. **Action:** Find an investment (e.g., starting a business, purchasing property) with potential for good returns.
   b. **Benefit:** Ensures borrowed funds are used to generate income.
2. **Research and Compare Loan Options**
   a. **Action:** Consult multiple lenders for the best interest rates and terms.
   b. **Benefit:** Reduces borrowing costs and repayment burden.
3. **Use a Loan Calculator**
   a. **Action:** Calculate monthly payments and total repayment amounts.
   b. **Benefit:** Understands long-term financial commitments.
4. **Assess Return on Investment (ROI)**
   a. **Action:** Project potential earnings and ensure they exceed loan costs.
   b. **Benefit:** Confirms the investment is financially viable.
5. **Plan for Contingencies**
   a. **Action:** Set aside emergency funds and consider risks.
   b. **Benefit:** Prepares for unexpected challenges without jeopardizing loan repayment.
6. **Avoid Predatory Lenders**
   a. **Action:** Steer clear of lenders with high interest rates and hidden fees.
   b. **Benefit:** Prevents falling into debt traps.
7. **Seek Professional Advice**
   a. **Action:** Discuss plans with financial advisors or mentors.
   b. **Benefit:** Gains expert insights and avoids common pitfalls.

Cinematic Bridge to Next Chapter

A month later, the expansion of Marcus's garage was complete. The newly constructed building stood tall, gleaming under the golden hues of the setting sun. The sign above read: **"Marcus's Automotive Empire"** in bold letters.

Marcus stood outside, hands on his hips, taking in the sight. The hum of activity surrounded him—mechanics buzzing around, customers admiring the upgraded facility, and the scent of fresh paint lingering in the air.

Selene approached, slipping her hand into his. "It's incredible, Marcus. Look at what you've built."

He turned to her, eyes reflecting a mix of pride and gratitude. "Couldn't have done it without yuh support, Selene. Taking that loan was a big step, but it opened doors mi never imagined."

She smiled warmly. "And now, with di business growing, wi can focus on making our money work even more for us."

He nodded. "Exactly. Saving alone got us this far, but it's time to unlock di magic of compound interest."

Jasmine joined them, holding up a flyer. "You two ready for the investment seminar next week? Time to learn how money can make more money."

Marcus grinned. "Absolutely. The journey to wealth building continues."

As the trio stood together, the camera pans out, capturing the vibrant scene of progress and the promise of greater things to come.

Stay tuned for Chapter 16: The Magic of Compound Interest—Why Saving Alone Isn't Enough

Chapter 16: The Magic of Compound Interest—Why Saving Alone Isn't Enough

Eye-Opening Seminar

The conference hall buzzed with energy as attendees filled the seats, conversations mingling with the soft hum of overhead lights. Marcus, Selene, and Jasmine settled into their spots near the front, eager for the seminar to begin.

"Mi nuh know 'bout unuh, but mi excited fi learn 'bout dis compound interest ting," Jasmine whispered, her eyes shining with anticipation.

"Same here. If wi can mek our money grow while wi sleep, dat's di real game-changer," Marcus agreed.

Selene glanced around. "Plenty people turned out. Clearly, others interested too."

A distinguished gentleman took the stage, his presence commanding attention. "Good evening, everyone. I'm Mr. Thompson, financial advisor and your guide into the world of investing and compound interest."

The room fell silent as he began.

"Many believe saving alone will secure their financial future. While saving is important, it's not enough. Tonight, we'll explore how compound interest can accelerate wealth-building."

Marcus leaned in, fully engrossed.

Understanding Compound Interest

Mr. Thompson projected a simple chart onto the screen. "Let's start wid di basics. Compound interest is earning interest on top of interest. It's di snowball effect of money growth."

He continued, "Imagine yuh invest J$100,000 at an annual interest rate of 10%. At di end of di first year, yuh earn J$10,000 in interest, totaling J$110,000. In di second year, yuh earn interest not just on di original J$100,000, but on di J$110,000. So, yuh earn J$11,000, and so on."

Selene whispered to Marcus, "So di interest keeps growing each year."

"Exactly. It's like planting a seed and watching it multiply," he replied.

Mr. Thompson displayed a table comparing simple interest and compound interest over 20 years.

Simple Interest (10% on J$100,000):

- Total Interest After 20 Years: J$200,000
- Total Amount: J$300,000

Compound Interest (10% annually on J$100,000):

- Total Interest After 20 Years: J$572,750
- Total Amount: J$672,750

"Yuh see di difference?" Mr. Thompson asked. "Compound interest more than doubles di returns compared to simple interest."

Jasmine's eyes widened. "Dat's impressive!"

The Power of Starting Early

"Time is your greatest ally when it comes to compound interest," Mr. Thompson emphasized. "Di earlier yuh start, di more significant di growth."

He illustrated with another example:

- **Person A** invests J$50,000 annually starting at age 25 and stops at age 35 (10 years, total investment J$500,000).
- **Person B** starts investing J$50,000 annually at age 35 and continues until age 65 (30 years, total investment J$1,500,000).

"Assuming an annual return of 8%, who do you think ends up with more money at age 65?" Mr. Thompson challenged.

Marcus scratched his head. "Probably Person B, since dem invest more over time."

Mr. Thompson smiled. "Actually, Person A ends up with more—about J$6.6 million compared to Person B's J$5.9 million. That's di magic of starting early and letting compound interest work over time."

Selene shook her head in amazement. "So starting early beats investing more later on."

"Precisely," Mr. Thompson affirmed.

Marcus and Selene's Investment Plan

Inspired, Marcus and Selene sat down that weekend to create their investment strategy.

"Wi need fi start now," Marcus declared. "No more delaying."

Selene nodded. "Agreed. Let's set clear goals."

Steps They Took:

1. **Defined Financial Goals**
   a. **Short-Term (1-3 years):** Save for wedding and emergency fund.
   b. **Medium-Term (3-7 years):** Invest in property.
   c. **Long-Term (10+ years):** Build retirement fund.
2. **Determined Investment Amount**
   a. **Monthly Investment:** J$30,000
3. **Chose Investment Vehicles**
   a. **Stocks and Mutual Funds:** Higher returns over long term.
   b. **Fixed Deposits and Bonds:** More stable, lower returns.
4. **Opened Investment Accounts**
   a. Set up accounts with reputable financial institutions.
5. **Automated Investments**
   a. Scheduled monthly transfers to investment accounts.

"By investing J$30,000 monthly at an average annual return of 8%, wi could have over J$15 million in 20 years," Selene calculated.

Marcus grinned. "Now that's wealth-building!"

Overcoming Doubts and Barriers

One evening, they met with Keisha and Junior to share their newfound knowledge.

"Mi love di idea, but mi barely have money left over after bills," Junior admitted.

Keisha agreed. "Investing sound good, but mi nuh know if mi can afford it."

Marcus encouraged them. "Even small amounts add up over time. Start wid what yuh can."

Selene added, "Plus, di discipline of investing regularly helps build wealth. Remember, 'One one cocoa full basket.'"

Junior brightened up. "Mi can start wid J$5,000 a month."

"Exactly! The key is consistency," Marcus affirmed.

Keisha smiled. "Alright, mi in. Time fi mek money work fi mi."

The Rule of 72

Back at Uncle Roy's veranda, the group gathered for more wisdom.

"Uncle Roy, wi learning 'bout compound interest and investing," Marcus shared enthusiastically.

He chuckled. "Ah, di secret of di wealthy. Let mi teach unuh 'bout di Rule of 72."

"What's dat?" Keisha asked.

"If yuh divide 72 by di annual interest rate, di result is di number of years it takes fi your money to double," Uncle Roy explained.

"For example, at 8% interest: 72 ÷ 8 = 9 years. So, it takes roughly 9 years fi your investment to double."

Selene's eyes widened. "That's a handy tool!"

"Indeed. It helps yuh understand di power of compound interest and make informed decisions," he nodded.

Mini Investment Challenge for Readers

Challenge: Start Investing and Harness the Power of Compound Interest

Step-by-Step Guide

1. **Set Clear Financial Goals**
    a. **Action:** Define what you want to achieve (e.g., retirement fund, home purchase).
    b. **Benefit:** Provides direction and motivation.
2. **Determine Your Investment Amount**
    a. **Action:** Decide on an amount you can invest regularly.
    b. **Benefit:** Consistency accelerates growth.
3. **Educate Yourself**
    a. **Action:** Learn about different investment options (stocks, bonds, mutual funds).
    b. **Benefit:** Makes informed choices that align with your goals and risk tolerance.
4. **Open an Investment Account**
    a. **Action:** Choose a reputable financial institution or brokerage.
    b. **Benefit:** Secure platform for your investments.
5. **Automate Your Investments**
    a. **Action:** Set up automatic transfers to your investment account.
    b. **Benefit:** Ensures discipline and regular contributions.
6. **Monitor and Rebalance**
    a. **Action:** Review your portfolio periodically and adjust as needed.
    b. **Benefit:** Keeps your investments aligned with your goals.

Outcome: By starting now, you leverage time and compound interest to build significant wealth over the long term.

Bridge to Next Chapter

As the months passed, Marcus and Selene watched their investments grow, albeit modestly at first.

"Look, our portfolio increased by 5% already," Selene noted one day.

"Every little bit counts. Imagine di growth over years," Marcus smiled.

One afternoon, Marcus received a call from Mr. Bennett.

"Marcus, I've heard about your expansion and investment ventures. Impressive progress," Mr. Bennett praised.

"Thank you, sir," Marcus replied.

"I have a proposition that could accelerate your financial growth even further. Perhaps we can discuss over dinner," Mr. Bennett suggested.

Marcus pondered the offer. "I wonder what he has in mind."

Selene looked at him thoughtfully. "Could be an opportunity to learn more about advanced investment strategies."

"Maybe it's time to explore how to plan for early retirement and true financial freedom," Marcus mused.

She nodded. "Agreed. Let's see where this leads."

Financial Lessons and Practical Takeaways

1. **Start Investing Early**
    a. **Action:** Begin investing as soon as possible, even with small amounts.
    b. **Takeaway:** Time amplifies the benefits of compound interest.
2. **Understand Compound Interest**
    a. **Action:** Learn how interest on interest accelerates growth.
    b. **Takeaway:** Recognizes the potential of investments over mere savings.

3. **Set Clear Financial Goals**
    a. **Action:** Define short-term, medium-term, and long-term objectives.
    b. **Takeaway:** Provides focus and a roadmap for investment strategies.
4. **Be Consistent**
    a. **Action:** Invest regularly, regardless of market fluctuations.
    b. **Takeaway:** Builds wealth steadily over time.
5. **Educate Yourself**
    a. **Action:** Continuously learn about investment options and financial tools.
    b. **Takeaway:** Empowers you to make informed decisions and adapt to changes.

Thoughts

The magic of compound interest lies in its ability to exponentially grow your wealth over time. Marcus and Selene's journey into investing demonstrates that with knowledge, discipline, and consistent action, financial dreams can become reality.

Stay tuned for Chapter 17: Investing 101—Making Your Money Work for You

Chapter 17: Investing 101—Making Your Money Work for You

A Proposal from Mr. Bennett

The golden hues of the setting sun bathed Kingston's skyline as Marcus adjusted his tie, nerves fluttering in his stomach. Selene stood beside him, radiating elegance in a sleek dress.

"Yuh ready?" she asked, her eyes reflecting his apprehension.

He exhaled slowly. "As ready as mi can be. Wonder what Mr. Bennett have up him sleeve."

They walked into the upscale restaurant, its ambiance a blend of modern chic and Caribbean flair. Mr. Bennett waved them over to a private table overlooking the city lights.

"Marcus, Selene, so glad you could make it," he greeted warmly.

"Good evening, Mr. Bennett," Marcus replied, taking a seat.

After light pleasantries and ordering dinner, Mr. Bennett leaned forward, his tone turning serious. "Marcus, your growth has been impressive. Your garage expansion shows vision and determination. But have you considered diversifying your investments?"

Marcus exchanged a glance with Selene. "Wi started investing in stocks and mutual funds recently. Trying fi build wealth over time."

Mr. Bennett smiled. "That's commendable. But I believe you have the potential to delve deeper—real estate, larger business ventures, perhaps even international markets."

Selene raised an eyebrow. "Those are big steps."

"Indeed," Mr. Bennett acknowledged. "But with the right guidance, the returns can be substantial. I'd like to offer you a mentorship and partnership opportunity."

Marcus felt a mix of excitement and caution. "What would that entail?"

"Join me in a new real estate development project on the north coast. It requires capital and expertise, and I believe you can contribute significantly," Mr. Bennett explained.

Weighing the Opportunity

That night, Marcus and Selene sat on their balcony, the gentle ocean breeze wrapping around them.

"Dis is huge, Selene. Getting into real estate could open new doors," Marcus mused.

"But it's also risky. Do we have the capital for such an investment?" she questioned.

"Wi could leverage some assets and consider financing options," he suggested.

She looked thoughtful. "Before jumping in, let's ensure we understand the ins and outs of these types of investments."

"Agreed. Maybe it's time wi deepen our knowledge on different investment vehicles," Marcus nodded.

Seeking Uncle Roy's Advice

The next day, they visited Uncle Roy, finding him tending to his flourishing vegetable garden.

"Uncle Roy, wi need fi pick yuh brain 'bout investing in real estate and other big ventures," Marcus began.

He wiped his hands and smiled. "Ah, stepping up in di investment world, I see."

"Mr. Bennett offered Marcus a partnership in a development project," Selene added.

Uncle Roy nodded slowly. "Real estate can be a solid investment, but it comes with its own challenges."

"That's why wi here—to understand di risks and benefits," Marcus said earnestly.

"Well, investing can take many forms—stocks, bonds, real estate, business ownership. Each has its own level of risk and potential returns," Uncle Roy explained.

He continued, "Real estate, for example, can provide steady income and appreciate over time, but it requires substantial capital and is less liquid than other investments."

"Mi hear that," Marcus agreed. "What about stocks versus bonds?"

"Stocks offer ownership in a company and can yield high returns, but they're volatile. Bonds are loans to entities like governments or corporations, offering lower returns but more stability," Uncle Roy elaborated.

Selene interjected, "And business ownership?"

"Well, that's where yuh own and operate a business—high potential for returns, but also high risk and demands on your time," Uncle Roy said.

"So how do wi decide what's best for us?" Marcus asked.

"Diversification is key. Don't put all your eggs in one basket. Spread your investments to balance risk and reward," Uncle Roy advised.

Educating Themselves

Back home, Marcus and Selene delved into research, books piled high on the coffee table, and financial websites open on their laptops.

"Look at this," Selene pointed at her screen. "Real estate investment trusts (REITs) allow you to invest in real estate without having to buy properties directly."

"Interesting. Less capital required and more liquidity," Marcus noted.

They listed potential investment avenues:

1. **Stocks and Mutual Funds**
   a. **Pros:** High return potential, easy to buy and sell.
   b. **Cons:** Volatile, requires market knowledge.
2. **Bonds**
   a. **Pros:** Steady income, lower risk.
   b. **Cons:** Lower returns compared to stocks.
3. **Real Estate**
   a. **Pros:** Tangible asset, rental income, appreciation.
   b. **Cons:** Requires capital, less liquid, property management hassles.
4. **Business Ventures**
   a. **Pros:** Control over operations, high return potential.
   b. **Cons:** High risk, time-consuming.
5. **REITs**

    a. **Pros:** Diversification in real estate, dividend income.

    b. **Cons:** Subject to market risks.

"Maybe wi can start by investing in REITs to get a feel for real estate investment without committing to a huge capital outlay," Selene suggested.

"Good idea. And perhaps consider Mr. Bennett's offer as a longer-term goal once wi have more experience," Marcus agreed.

A Meeting with Jasmine

They met with Jasmine at a local café to discuss their thoughts.

"Moving into different investment areas is smart," Jasmine encouraged. "But remember to assess your risk tolerance and investment horizon."

"True. Wi nuh want fi overextend ourselves," Marcus agreed.

"Also, have you considered investing in small businesses or startups? Supporting local entrepreneurs can be rewarding," Jasmine proposed.

Selene smiled. "That's a great point. It aligns with our values of community growth."

"And there's potential for significant returns if di business takes off," Jasmine added.

"Wi can allocate a portion of our investment funds towards that," Marcus nodded.

Making Informed Decisions

Marcus and Selene decided to:

1. **Diversify Their Portfolio:**

  a. Allocate investments across stocks, bonds, real estate (REITs), and small businesses.
2. **Set Investment Percentages:**
  a. **Stocks and Mutual Funds:** 40%
  b. **Bonds:** 20%
  c. **REITs:** 20%
  d. **Small Business Investments:** 10%
  e. **Emergency Fund and Cash Reserves:** 10%
3. **Continue Financial Education:**
  a. Attend workshops, read books, and engage with financial advisors.

"By spreading out our investments, wi reduce risk and increase opportunities for returns," Selene stated.

"Exactly. And as wi grow more comfortable, wi can adjust our strategy," Marcus agreed.

The Importance of Due Diligence

Uncle Roy visited them, bringing along a folder of articles.

"Mi glad unuh taking investment seriously. But remember, due diligence is crucial," he emphasized.

"What's that?" Keisha asked, joining the conversation.

"Due diligence is thoroughly researching any investment before committing your money. Understand di business model, financial health, market conditions, and potential risks," Uncle Roy explained.

Marcus nodded. "So before investing in a small business, wi need fi review their business plan, financial statements, and market potential."

"Exactly. Never invest blindly based on promises of high returns," Uncle Roy warned.

Selene added, "And for stocks, wi should look at the company's performance, industry trends, and management."

Mini Investment Action Plan for Readers

Action Plan: Begin Your Investment Journey

Step-by-Step Guide

1. **Assess Your Financial Situation**
    a. **Action:** Evaluate your income, expenses, debts, and savings.
    b. **Benefit:** Determines how much you can invest without financial strain.
2. **Set Investment Goals**
    a. **Action:** Define clear, measurable objectives (e.g., retirement, buying a home, education fund).
    b. **Benefit:** Guides your investment choices and strategies.
3. **Determine Your Risk Tolerance**
    a. **Action:** Understand how much risk you're willing to take.
    b. **Benefit:** Ensures your investments align with your comfort level.
4. **Educate Yourself**
    a. **Action:** Learn about different investment options and how they work.
    b. **Benefit:** Empowers you to make informed decisions.
5. **Start Small**
    a. **Action:** Begin with modest investments to gain experience.
    b. **Benefit:** Minimizes risk while you learn.
6. **Diversify Your Portfolio**
    a. **Action:** Spread investments across various asset classes.
    b. **Benefit:** Reduces risk and enhances potential returns.
7. **Monitor and Adjust**

a. **Action:** Regularly review your investments and adjust as needed.
b. **Benefit:** Keeps your portfolio aligned with your goals.

Embracing the Journey

A few months later, Marcus and Selene had diversified their investments and were seeing positive results. They attended networking events, connected with other entrepreneurs, and continued learning.

One evening, as they stood on the balcony overlooking the city lights, Marcus mused, "It's amazing how far wi come. From struggling wid budgeting to now having a growing investment portfolio."

Selene squeezed his hand. "And it's only the beginning. Wi making our money work for us, and setting up a legacy for our future family."

He smiled. "Indeed. Financial freedom is within reach."

Just then, Marcus's phone buzzed with a message from Mr. Bennett: "Opportunity awaits. Let's discuss your next big move."

Marcus looked at Selene. "Seems like it's time to consider bigger ventures."

She nodded confidently. "We're ready."

Bridge to Next Chapter

As they prepared for the meeting with Mr. Bennett, Marcus reflected on the journey so far.

"Wi learned 'bout investing, diversified our portfolio, and now we're being presented with even greater opportunities," he said.

"Yes, but wi must ensure we plan wisely for the future," Selene reminded him.

"Agreed. Perhaps it's time to delve deeper into planning for early retirement and achieving true financial freedom," Marcus suggested.

She smiled. "Then let's make that our next step."

Financial Lessons and Practical Takeaways

1. **Diversify Investments**
   a. **Action:** Spread your investments across different assets like stocks, bonds, real estate, and businesses.
   b. **Takeaway:** Diversification reduces risk and increases potential for returns.
2. **Do Your Due Diligence**
   a. **Action:** Research thoroughly before investing.
   b. **Takeaway:** Informed decisions protect you from unnecessary risks.
3. **Assess Risk Tolerance**
   a. **Action:** Understand your comfort level with investment risks.
   b. **Takeaway:** Aligns your investments with your financial goals and peace of mind.
4. **Invest in Financial Education**
   a. **Action:** Continuously learn about investing and financial strategies.
   b. **Takeaway:** Knowledge empowers you to make better investment choices.
5. **Start Small and Grow**
   a. **Action:** Begin investing with amounts you can afford and increase over time.
   b. **Takeaway:** Builds confidence and experience in managing investments.

Thoughts

Investing is a powerful tool for building wealth and achieving financial independence. Marcus and Selene's journey shows that with careful planning, education, and diversification, anyone can make their money work for them.

Stay tuned for Chapter 18: Financial Freedom—How to Plan for Early Retirement

Chapter 19: Protecting Your Wealth—Understanding Insurance & Estate Planning

A Harsh Wake-Up Call

The vibrant streets of Kingston bustled as Marcus drove towards the garage. His phone rang, and seeing Junior's name, he answered cheerfully.

"Junior! Wha gwaan, mi bredda?" Marcus greeted.

Silence hung on the other end for a moment before Junior's strained voice came through. "Marcus, mi inna big trouble."

Marcus's smile faded. "What happen? Everything alright?"

"Mi father got seriously ill sudden. Di medical bills piling up, and wi nuh have insurance fi cover it. Mi nuh know what fi do," Junior confessed, his voice cracking.

Marcus felt a knot tighten in his stomach. "Jah know, mi sorry fi hear dat. Is there anything mi can do fi help?"

"Anything yuh can assist with would mean di world. Mi just... mi never expect dis. It draining all wi savings, and mi close to losing di house," Junior admitted.

Marcus's mind raced. "Alright, link up later and wi see how wi can support."

As he hung up, Marcus couldn't shake the unease. The reality of unforeseen events wiping out finances hit hard.

The Importance of Health Insurance

That evening, Marcus and Selene sat together, the weight of Junior's situation heavy on their minds.

"Selene, yuh see how one medical emergency can mash up years of savings?" Marcus remarked.

She nodded solemnly. "It's frightening. And many people nuh have health insurance because dem think it's too expensive or unnecessary."

"Wi need fi ensure wi nuh fall into dat trap. Mi nuh want to burden anyone if sickness strikes," he stated.

"Agreed. Let's look into health insurance options," Selene suggested.

They researched local health insurance plans, comparing coverage and costs.

"Look yah, dis plan covers major medical emergencies and hospitalization, and di premium is reasonable," Selene pointed out.

Marcus nodded. "It's an investment in our peace of mind. Wi should sign up as soon as possible."

When Disaster Strikes

A few weeks later, news spread that Mr. Hinds, a fellow business owner in the community, had lost his shop to a fire. Marcus and Selene attended a community meeting organized to support him.

Mr. Hinds stood before the crowd, tears welling in his eyes. "Mi never think dis would happen to me. In di blink of an eye, mi livelihood gone. And mi never insure di building or mi stock."

Murmurs of sympathy rippled through the crowd.

Jasmine whispered to Marcus, "Dis show how important it is fi protect wi business assets."

Marcus felt a chill. "True. Imagine if dat happen to di garage."

Selene squeezed his hand. "Wi can't leave things to chance. Wi need fi get proper insurance fi di business."

Learning About Different Types of Insurance

Determined to act, Marcus and Selene met with Mr. Edwards, their trusted lawyer, to discuss their options.

"Mr. Edwards, wi realize wi need fi protect ourselves and our assets better. Can you guide us through di different types of insurance and estate planning?" Marcus asked.

Mr. Edwards smiled. "Absolutely. It's wise to consider these things before any misfortune strikes."

He began explaining:

1. Health Insurance

- **Purpose:** Covers medical expenses due to illness or injury.
- **Options:** Individual plans, family plans, employer-provided plans.
- **Advice:** Choose a plan that offers comprehensive coverage within your budget.

2. Life Insurance

- **Purpose:** Provides financial support to beneficiaries upon the policyholder's death.
- **Types:**

- ○ **Term Life Insurance:** Coverage for a specific period; lower premiums; no cash value.
  - ○ **Whole Life Insurance:** Lifetime coverage; higher premiums; accumulates cash value.
- **Advice:** Term life is often sufficient and more affordable for most people's needs.

3. Property Insurance (Home & Business)

- **Purpose:** Protects against loss or damage to property due to events like fire, theft, or natural disasters.
- **Advice:** Ensure coverage includes building and contents; consider additional coverage for specific risks prevalent in your area.

4. Liability Insurance

- **Purpose:** Protects against legal claims for injury or damage caused to others on your property or by your business operations.
- **Advice:** Essential for business owners to safeguard against lawsuits.

5. Business Interruption Insurance

- **Purpose:** Covers loss of income during periods when business operations are disrupted due to covered perils.
- **Advice:** Helps maintain cash flow during recovery periods.

6. Critical Illness Insurance

- **Purpose:** Provides a lump-sum payment upon diagnosis of specified serious illnesses.
- **Advice:** Can alleviate financial strain during prolonged medical treatments.

Estate Planning and Generational Wealth

Mr. Edwards continued, "Beyond insurance, estate planning is crucial for passing on wealth to your loved ones."

"Wi heard about wills and trusts, but not sure how they work," Selene admitted.

Mr. Edwards explained:

1. Wills

- **Purpose:** Legal document stating how your assets should be distributed after death.
- **Advice:** Keep it updated; appoint a trustworthy executor.

2. Trusts

- **Purpose:** Allows a third party (trustee) to manage assets on behalf of beneficiaries.
- **Types:**
    - **Living Trust:** Established during your lifetime; can help avoid probate.
    - **Testamentary Trust:** Created upon death according to the will.
- **Advice:** Useful for managing assets for minors or reducing estate taxes.

3. Power of Attorney

- **Purpose:** Legal document allowing someone to make decisions on your behalf if you're incapacitated.
- **Advice:** Assign to someone you trust implicitly.

4. Beneficiary Designations

- **Purpose:** Specifies who receives assets like life insurance proceeds or retirement accounts.
- **Advice:** Regularly review and update to reflect life changes.

5. Estate Taxes

- **Advice:** Plan ahead to minimize taxes and ensure more assets pass to beneficiaries.

Taking Action

"Wi need fi get all these things in order," Marcus declared.

"Agreed. Let's start by getting proper insurance coverage for ourselves and di business," Selene responded.

They contacted an insurance broker who helped them:

- **Secure Health Insurance:** Comprehensive plan covering major medical needs.
- **Obtain Life Insurance:** Term life policies sufficient to support each other and future children.
- **Insure the Business and Home:** Coverage against fire, theft, natural disasters, and liability.
- **Explore Critical Illness Insurance:** For added protection against serious health issues.

Next, they worked with Mr. Edwards to:

- **Draft Wills:** Clearly outlining asset distribution and appointing executors.
- **Set Up a Living Trust:** To manage assets efficiently and provide for family members.
- **Assign Powers of Attorney:** For financial and medical decisions if needed.

A Conversation with Junior

A few weeks later, Marcus met with Junior, who looked more relieved.

"Marcus, mi appreciate all di support. Things slowly getting better," Junior said gratefully.

"Happy fi hear dat. Have yuh thought about setting up insurance fi yuh family?" Marcus asked.

Junior sighed. "Mi realize how important it is now. Mi nuh want to be caught off guard again."

"Mi can link yuh with mi insurance broker and lawyer fi help set things up," Marcus offered.

Junior nodded. "That would be great. Time fi protect what little wi have and plan fi di future."

Mini Wealth Protection Checklist for Readers

Action Plan: Protect Your Wealth and Secure Your Legacy

Step-by-Step Guide

1. **Assess Your Insurance Needs**
   a. **Action:** Review your current coverage and identify gaps.
   b. **Benefit:** Ensures you're adequately protected against potential risks.
2. **Secure Health Insurance**
   a. **Action:** Choose a plan that fits your needs and budget.
   b. **Benefit:** Prevents medical expenses from depleting your wealth.
3. **Obtain Life Insurance**

a. **Action:** Decide between term and whole life insurance based on your situation.
b. **Benefit:** Provides financial security for your loved ones.

4. **Insure Property and Assets**
    a. **Action:** Get coverage for your home, vehicle, and business.
    b. **Benefit:** Protects against loss from disasters, theft, or accidents.

5. **Consider Liability Insurance**
    a. **Action:** Add coverage to protect against legal claims.
    b. **Benefit:** Shields your assets from lawsuits.

6. **Plan Your Estate**
    a. **Action:** Draft a will, set up trusts if necessary, and assign powers of attorney.
    b. **Benefit:** Ensures your assets are distributed according to your wishes and reduces family disputes.

7. **Regularly Review and Update Plans**
    a. **Action:** Update your insurance policies and estate documents as life changes occur.
    b. **Benefit:** Keeps your protection strategies aligned with your current circumstances.

Encouragement: Don't leave your hard-earned wealth vulnerable. Take proactive steps to safeguard your future and provide peace of mind for yourself and your family.

Bridging to the Final Chapter

One evening, as Marcus and Selene relaxed after a long day, Selene mused, "We've learned so much on this journey—about making money, growing it, and now protecting it."

"Indeed. But there's one more step wi need fi focus on—ensuring that our wealth outlives us and benefits future generations," Marcus responded.

"Leaving a legacy," Selene smiled. "Time to think about generational wealth."

"Exactly. Let's delve into how we can make sure our money works for our children's children," Marcus agreed.

Financial Lessons and Practical Takeaways

1. **Importance of Insurance**
    a. **Action:** Secure various insurance policies to protect against unexpected events.
    b. **Takeaway:** Insurance safeguards your wealth and prevents financial ruin due to unforeseen circumstances.
2. **Understanding Different Insurance Types**
    a. **Action:** Learn about health, life, property, liability, and business insurance.
    b. **Takeaway:** Each type offers specific protections essential for comprehensive coverage.
3. **Estate Planning Essentials**
    a. **Action:** Create wills, trusts, and assign powers of attorney.
    b. **Takeaway:** Ensures your assets are distributed according to your wishes and reduces potential conflicts.
4. **Regularly Update Plans**
    a. **Action:** Review and adjust insurance and estate documents as life changes occur.
    b. **Takeaway:** Keeps your protection strategies effective and relevant.
5. **Educate and Encourage Others**
    a. **Action:** Share knowledge about wealth protection with family and friends.

b.   **Takeaway:** Builds a financially secure community and supports collective well-being.

Thoughts

Protecting your wealth through insurance and estate planning is a crucial aspect of financial management. Marcus and Selene's proactive approach highlights the peace of mind that comes from knowing you're prepared for life's uncertainties and have secured your legacy for future generations.

Stay tuned for the final chapter: Chapter 20: Legacy and Generational Wealth—Mek Sure Yuh Money Outlive Yuh

Chapter 20: Legacy and Generational Wealth—Mek Sure Yuh Money Outlive Yuh

Reflecting on the Journey

The warm Jamaican sun cast its golden hue over Marcus and Selene's backyard as they hosted a family gathering. Laughter filled the air as children played, and the aroma of jerk chicken wafted from the grill. Marcus watched the scene with a serene smile.

"Remember when we started dis journey?" he mused to Selene, who stood beside him.

She nodded, her eyes reflecting the joy of the moment. "From budgeting to building wealth, to now thinking 'bout how wi can leave a lasting legacy."

"Wi come a long way," Marcus agreed. "But now, it's time fi ensure that all we've worked for benefits not just us, but future generations."

Teaching the Next Generation

Later that afternoon, Marcus gathered the children, including his niece and nephew, under the shade of the mango tree.

"Uncle Marcus, tell us a story!" his niece, Aaliyah, exclaimed.

He grinned. "Alright, but dis story is 'bout money and how fi make it work fi you."

They listened intently as he simplified financial concepts.

"Yuh see, money is like a seed. If yuh plant it and take care of it, it grows into a big tree that bears fruit for years to come," he explained.

"How do we plant money?" his nephew, Troy, asked eagerly.

"By saving and investing. And by learning how money works," Marcus replied. "The earlier yuh start, the bigger di tree grows."

Selene joined them, adding, "And it's important to share and help others. Wealth is not just 'bout what you have, but what you can do for others."

Setting Up Generational Wealth Structures

In the weeks that followed, Marcus and Selene met with Mr. Edwards to establish plans for transferring their wealth to future generations.

1. Trust Funds for Education

- **Action:** Set up trust funds dedicated to their children's and nieces' and nephews' education.
- **Benefit:** Ensures funds are used for educational purposes, promoting long-term success.

2. Family Investment Portfolio

- **Action:** Create a family investment portfolio managed collectively.
- **Benefit:** Teaches financial responsibility and investment skills to younger family members.

3. Real Estate Holdings

- **Action:** Acquire rental properties to generate steady income.
- **Benefit:** Provides ongoing revenue streams and appreciating assets to pass down.

4. Life Insurance Policies with Estate Planning

- **Action:** Structure life insurance to fund trusts upon passing.
- **Benefit:** Provides liquidity to cover estate taxes and support beneficiaries.

5. Business Succession Plan

- **Action:** Develop a plan for transferring ownership and management of the garage to a trusted family member or partner.
- **Benefit:** Ensures the continued success of the business beyond their involvement.

Avoiding Common Mistakes

One evening, Uncle Roy shared stories of families who lost generational wealth due to poor planning.

"Mi see cases where wealth disappear because di next generation nuh know how fi manage it," he cautioned.

"How can we prevent dat?" Selene asked.

"Education is key. Teach dem young 'bout financial literacy, hard work, and responsibility," Uncle Roy advised.

Marcus added, "We should also set up structures dat protect di assets, like trusts and proper legal frameworks."

Uncle Roy nodded. "And avoid di pitfalls of greed and entitlement. Make sure they understand di value of money and di importance of maintaining it."

Giving Back to the Community

Marcus and Selene believed that true legacy included uplifting others.

Community Initiatives:

1. **Mentorship Programs**
   a. **Action:** Establish mentorship opportunities for young entrepreneurs.
   b. **Benefit:** Empowers the next generation with knowledge and support.
2. **Scholarships**
   a. **Action:** Fund educational scholarships for underprivileged youth.
   b. **Benefit:** Provides access to education for those who might not afford it otherwise.
3. **Community Development Projects**
   a. **Action:** Invest in local infrastructure projects, such as community centers and libraries.
   b. **Benefit:** Enhances the quality of life in their community.
4. **Financial Literacy Workshops**
   a. **Action:** Host free workshops teaching budgeting, saving, and investing.
   b. **Benefit:** Promotes financial empowerment within the community.

A Family Meeting

Marcus and Selene organized a family meeting to discuss their plans.

"Wi want to share with unuh how we plan fi secure our family's future," Marcus began.

They outlined their generational wealth strategies, emphasizing the importance of financial education.

"Wi also expect each of you to take an active role in learning and contributing," Selene added.

Aaliyah raised her hand. "Will you teach us how to invest too?"

"Absolutely," Marcus smiled. "Wi'll have regular family sessions to learn and make decisions together."

The Final Reflection

Standing on a hillside overlooking the twinkling lights of Kingston, Marcus and Selene contemplated their journey.

"From facing financial struggles to building a thriving business and investment portfolio," Marcus reminisced.

"And now, setting up a legacy that will impact generations," Selene added.

"Mi realize that wealth is not just 'bout money. It's 'bout knowledge, values, and di positive impact wi have on others," Marcus said thoughtfully.

Selene nodded. "And ensuring that those who come after us are equipped to carry it forward."

He turned to her, a profound sense of fulfillment in his eyes. "Wi did good, Selene."

She smiled warmly. "Yes, Marcus. Wi did."

Financial Lessons and Practical Takeaways

1. **Educate the Next Generation**

a. **Action:** Teach children and young family members about money management and investment.

   b. **Takeaway:** Financial literacy is crucial for preserving and growing wealth across generations.

2. **Establish Trusts and Legal Structures**

   a. **Action:** Set up trusts and legal entities to manage and protect assets.

   b. **Takeaway:** Proper structures ensure assets are used according to your wishes and protected from mismanagement.

3. **Create a Succession Plan**

   a. **Action:** Plan for the transfer of business ownership and responsibilities.

   b. **Takeaway:** Smooth transitions maintain business continuity and success.

4. **Promote Family Involvement**

   a. **Action:** Involve family members in financial decisions and operations.

   b. **Takeaway:** Encourages responsibility and prepares the next generation to take over.

5. **Give Back to the Community**

   a. **Action:** Engage in philanthropy and community development.

   b. **Takeaway:** Builds a legacy of impact beyond personal wealth, enriching the lives of others.

6. **Avoid Wealth Destruction Pitfalls**

   a. **Action:** Educate heirs, avoid excessive gifting without accountability, and instill strong values.

   b. **Takeaway:** Prevents the erosion of wealth through misuse or lack of appreciation.

Final Scene: Inspiring Others

At a community event, Marcus took the stage to address a crowd of aspiring entrepreneurs and families.

"Mi stand here not just as a businessman, but as someone who believes in di power of knowledge and planning," he began.

He shared his journey, the lessons learned, and the importance of thinking long-term.

"Building wealth is one ting, but ensuring it outlives you is another. Invest in education—both financial and moral—for di next generation. Let's create legacies dat uplift not just our families but our entire community."

Thunderous applause erupted as he concluded.

Epilogue

Years later, the Thomas family legacy thrived. The garage had expanded into multiple locations, the family investment portfolio flourished, and their community initiatives transformed countless lives.

Aaliyah, now a confident young woman, stood where Marcus once did, mentoring the next wave of entrepreneurs.

"Mi grandparents taught me that wealth is not just what you have, but what you do with it," she said passionately.

The torch had been passed, the legacy continued.

Final Thoughts

Building a lasting legacy requires foresight, dedication, and a commitment to empowering others. Marcus and Selene's journey from financial uncertainty to generational wealth exemplifies the transformative power of knowledge, strategic planning, and heartfelt giving.

Your Journey Begins Now

As you close this book, remember that financial empowerment is within your reach. Apply the lessons learned, embrace the challenges, and take proactive steps toward securing not just your financial future, but that of generations to come.

Mek wi continue fi mek money talk—wisely, purposefully, and with heart.

Acknowledgments

To all the readers committed to transforming their financial lives, may this book serve as a guide and inspiration. Remember, every journey starts with a single step—take yours today.

A special thank you to Chinelle Spencer, FCCA, CA, for her unparalleled guidance and support. Your expertise and dedication to financial excellence have been a constant source of inspiration. Your innovative approaches to financial solutions continue to illuminate the path forward for countless individuals and businesses.

About the Main Charachters

Marcus and Selene Thomas are fictional representations of countless individuals striving for financial empowerment. Their story encapsulates real-life experiences, wisdom, and cultural richness. The "Money Mek Wi Talk" series aims to provide practical financial guidance woven into engaging narratives that resonate with readers from all walks of life.

Thank you for joining us on this journey. Stay tuned for more in the "Money Mek Wi Talk" series, where we delve deeper into advanced investment strategies, entrepreneurship, and global financial opportunities.

Conclusion: Money Mek Wi Talk, But Knowledge Mek Wi Win

Money deh out deh. But if yuh nuh know how fi **earn, manage, invest, and protect it**, di system will eat yuh alive.

Wi come from a culture of **resilience, hustle, and big dreams**—but too often, nobody teach wi di **rules of wealth.**

Now, yuh have di knowledge. **Use it. Apply it. Share it.**

Remember: **Wealth is not just money. It's freedom.** 🚀

Are yuh ready fi level up?

📣 Join Wi Community! (Stay Connected & Learn More)

✅ 📕 **FREE Patois Financial Literacy Course:**

🎓 patwah.unschooler.me

✅ 🖥️ **Financial & Business Blog on Medium:**

📖 https://medium.com/@Real_Jamaican_Patois_or_Patwah

✅ 📖 **My Author Page (More Books & Resources):**

📚 amazon.com/author/marvin-buckley

📌 Follow mi fi **more knowledge, real-life strategies, and financial empowerment.**

🔥 **Now, go out deh and BUILD GENERATIONAL WEALTH!** 🔥

🔊 Bonus Section: Financial Tools & Resources

Recommended Books & Courses:

- 📖 *Rich Dad Poor Dad* by Robert Kiyosaki
- 📖 *The Richest Man in Babylon* by George S. Clason
- 📖 *The Intelligent Investor* by Benjamin Graham

Financial Planning Apps:

- Mint (Budgeting)
- Robinhood (Investing)
- YNAB (You Need A Budget)

Real Estate Investment Resources:

- BiggerPockets.com (Community for real estate investors)
- Investopedia (Free investment education)

🚀 **Next Step:** Wi giving yuh di blueprint—**now is time fi ACTION!**

Final Author Bio

📌 **About the Author: Marvin Buckley**

Marvin Buckley is a **Jamaican entrepreneur** dedicated to **helping people achieve financial independence.**

With real-life experience **building businesses, investing, and teaching financial literacy**, Marvin believes in **making financial knowledge accessible through relatable, easy-to-apply lessons.**

🔥 **Connect With Marvin:**

📚 More Books: amazon.com/author/marvin-buckley
📖 Medium Blog:
https://medium.com/@Real_Jamaican_Patois_or_Patwah
🎓 Free Course: patwah.unschooler.me

✉ **For business inquiries, workshops, and collaborations:**
patwah@sharksolutions.info

About the Accountant: Chinelle Spencer

Chinelle Spencer, FCCA, CA Visionary Leader in Global Asset Management and Public Accounting

Chinelle Spencer is a highly accomplished Chartered Accountant (FCCA, CA) with over a decade of experience, spanning across multiple global Big 4 firms in three countries, including the financial powerhouse of the Cayman Islands. Specializing in asset management, Chinelle has established a reputation for her innovative approaches to financial solutions, helping businesses and individuals navigate complex financial landscapes with precision and insight.

Now the founder and managing partner of her own public accounting firm, Chinelle continues to drive change, leveraging her extensive expertise to offer strategic financial consulting, risk management, and audit services. Her trajectory from international financial hubs to leading her own practice is a testament to her ambition, unwavering professionalism, and forward-thinking leadership.

Email: contact@primaxjm.com **Contact #:** (876) 990-1985 **Website:** https://www.primaxjm.com